TINY TRAINS

Britain's Miniature Railways

2024-2025

EDITOR
John Robinson

Fourteenth Edition

FOREWORD & ACKNOWLEDGEMENTS

Following a 5-year hiatus which was caused mainly by the Covid pandemic lockdown and its aftermath, we are pleased to be able to re-launch Tiny Trains.

We were greatly impressed by the friendly and cooperative manner of the members and helpers of the railways which we selected to appear in this book, and wish to thank them all for the help that they have given. In addition we wish to thank Bob Budd (cover design), Michael Robinson (page layouts) and Jonathan James (who provided a number of photographs) for their help.

Although we believe that the information contained in this guide is accurate at the time of going to press, we, and the Railways and Museums itemised, are unable to accept liability for any loss, damage, distress or injury suffered as a result of any inaccuracies. Furthermore, we and the Railways are unable to guarantee operating and opening times which may always be subject to cancellation without notice, particularly during adverse weather conditions.

The cover photograph was taken in 2023 at the Little Western Railway which is the oldest 7¼ inch railway in Cornwall and is located within the beautiful 24 acre Trenance Leisure Park and Gardens, in Newquay.

John Robinson

EDITOR

British Library Cataloguing in Publication Data
A catalogue record for this book is available from the British Library

ISBN-13:   978-1-86223-516-8

Manufactured in the UK by 4edge Ltd

CONTENTS

ABBEY PARK MINIATURE RAILWAY

Address: Abbey Park, Leicester LE1 3EJ
Telephone Nº: (0116) 247-9844
Year Formed: 1909 (located at Abbey Park since 1951)
Location of Line: Victorian Public Park
Length of Line: 874 yards

Nº of Steam Locos: Members locos only
Nº of Other Locos: 6 diesels
Approx Nº of Visitors P.A.: 11,000
Gauges: 2½ inches, 3½ inches, 5 inches and 7¼ inches (Also '0' and '1' gauge)
Web site: www.ismeabbeypark.com

GENERAL INFORMATION

Nearest Mainline Station: Leicester (1½ miles)
Nearest Bus Station: Leicester (½ mile)
Car Parking: Available at the nearby Riverside Car Park (Pay and Display)
Coach Parking: None
Souvenir Shop(s): None
Food & Drinks: Available elsewhere in the Park

SPECIAL INFORMATION

The railway is operated by the Leicester Society of Model Engineers.

OPERATING INFORMATION

Opening Times: 2024 dates: Sundays and Bank Holiday Mondays from 24th March until 27th October. Also open on Wednesdays during the local school holidays. Santa Specials will operate on 8th December – prior booking is essential.
Trains run from 1.00pm to 5.00pm.
Steam Working: Subject to availability, otherwise diesel services.
Prices: Adults £1.50
Children £1.50 (Under-5s ride for free)

Detailed Directions by Car:
From All Parts: The railway is located at the South-Western edge of Leicester's Abbey Park and is best accessed from the St. Margaret's Riverside car park, situated off the A6 (North) St. Margaret's Way, adjoining the inner ring-road (Burley's Way). The station is located towards the riverside end of Cave's Walk, Abbey Park.

ABBEYDALE MINIATURE RAILWAY

Address: Abbeydale Road South, Sheffield S17 3LB	**Nº of Steam Locos:** 10+
Year Formed: 1900 (Operating in the current location since 1978)	**Nº of Other Locos:** 8+
	Approx Nº of Visitors P.A.: 18,000+
	Gauges: 2½ inches, 3½ inches, 5 inches
Location of Line: Abbeydale Road South	and 7¼ inches
Length of Line: 1,000 yards ground-level, 200 yards elevated	**Web:** www.sheffieldmodelengineers.com

GENERAL INFORMATION

Nearest Mainline Station: Dore & Totley (200 yards)
Nearest Bus Station: Sheffield (4½ miles). The 97, 98 and 218 bus services stop outside the railway.
Car Parking: Limited spaces available on site
Coach Parking: Street parking only
Souvenir Shop(s): Yes
Food & Drinks: Available

SPECIAL INFORMATION

The Railway is operated by the Sheffield and District Society of Model and Experimental Engineers. The railway itself is located very close to the historical Abbeydale Industrial Hamlet, a unique 18th Century industrial works and one of the largest water-powered sites on the River Sheaf.

OPERATING INFORMATION

Opening Times: 2024 dates: 10th & 24th March; 14th & 28th April; 12th & 26th May; 9th & 23rd June; 14th & 28th July; 11th & 25th August; 8th & 22nd September; 6th & 20th October.
Also open 8th & 15th December for Santa Specials. Please check the web site for further details.
Usual opening hours are 1.00pm to 5.00pm.
Steam Working: Most operating days.
Prices: £2.00 per ride (except Santa Specials)

Detailed Directions by Car:
From the South: Exit the M1 at Junction 29 and take the A617 to Chesterfield. Then take the A61 towards Sheffield until you reach the Meadowhead roundabout on the outskirts of Sheffield. Take the first exit signposted A621 to Bakewell, then bear right. Follow signs to Bakewell & Abbeydale Industrial Hamlet. The railway entrance is on the right 200 yards past the Hamlet; From the North and East: Exit the M1 at Junction 33 and take the A630 towards Sheffield. After about 4 miles join the A6102 (Prince of Wales Road). Follow the A6102 (outer ring road) until you reach the Meadowhead roundabout (A61). Take the 2nd exit signposted A621 to Bakewell, then as above; From the West: Take the A621 to Sheffield. Pass through Totley then look out for Dore and Totley Station on your right. The railway entrance is on the left after about 150 yards.

ASHTON COURT ESTATE MINIATURE RAILWAY

Address: Ashton Court Estate, Long Ashton, North Somerset   BS8 3PX
Telephone Nº: (0117) 946-7110
Year Formed: Opened 1973
Location of Line: Ashton Court Estate
Length of Line: Two tracks, each approximately a third of a mile in length

Nº of Steam Locos: 3
Nº of Other Locos: 5
Approx Nº of Visitors P.A.: 30,000
Gauge: 3½ inches, 5 inches & 7¼ inches
Website: www.bristolmodelengineers.co.uk

GENERAL INFORMATION

Nearest Mainline Station: Bristol Temple Meads (Approximately 5 miles)
Nearest Bus Station: Bristol (4 miles)
Car Parking: Pay and Display adjacent to the site
Coach Parking: Available by prior arrangement
Souvenir Shop(s): None
Food & Drinks: None

SPECIAL INFORMATION

The Railway is owned and operated by the Bristol Society of Model & Experimental Engineers which was founded in 1909.

OPERATING INFORMATION

Opening Times: 2024 dates: 31st March; 14th & 21st April; 5th, 6th, 26th & 27th May; 9th, 16th & 30th June; 7th, 21st & 28th July; 25th & 26th August; 8th, 15th & 29th September; 6th, 20th & 27th October and Santa Specials on 8th December (pre-booking required). Trains run from 12.00pm to 5.00pm, weather permitting.
Steam Working: All operating days.
Prices: £1.75p per ride per person. Also 5 tickets are available for £7.50
Note: Tickets for the very popular Santa Specials are £11.00 pre-bookable from 28th July.

Detailed Directions by Car:
Exit the M5 at junction 19 and take the A369 towards Bristol. After approximately 6 miles, just past the B3129 traffic lights is Ashton Court Estate. However, there is no right turn from this direction. Instead, take the side road on the left (North Road), turn right into Bridge Road and continue straight across the A369 at the traffic lights into the Clifton Lodge Entrance. Take the first right then the first right again before the golf kiosk car park.

AVONVALE MODEL ENGINEERING SOCIETY

Address: Hillers, Heath Farm, Alcester
Warwickshire   B49 5PD
Phone Nº: 07745- 222003
Year Formed: 2001
Location of Line: Hillers, Dunnington
Length of Line: A third of a mile

Nº of Steam Locos: 16
Nº of Other Locos: 12
Approx Nº of Visitors P.A.: 3,000
Gauge: 5 inches and 7¼ inches
Website: www.avonvale.me.uk

GENERAL INFORMATION

Nearest Mainline Station: Evesham (11 miles)
Nearest Bus Station: Stratford-upon-Avon (13 miles)
Car Parking: Free parking available on site
Coach Parking: None
Souvenir Shop(s): None
Food & Drinks: Available

SPECIAL INFORMATION

The Engines are all privately owned and run as required. The railway is located at Hillers where other attractions include a Café, a Farm Shop and a Display Garden.

OPERATING INFORMATION

Opening Times: 2024 dates: 30th & 31st March; 13th, 14th, 27th & 28th April; 4th, 5th, 25th & 26th May; 8th, 9th, 22nd & 23rd June; 6th, 7th, 20th & 21st July; 3rd, 4th, 24th & 25th August; 7th, 8th, 21st & 22nd September; 5th, 6th, 26th & 27th October. Trains run from 11.00am to 4.00pm.
Steam Working: Where possible at least two steam locos run on each operating day.
Prices: £1.00 per ride per person on normal days
8 tickets cost £7.00

Detailed Directions by Car:
From the North: Take the A435 or A46 to Alcester then follow the B4088 to Dunnington. Once in Dunnington, turn right at the crossroad and Hillers is on the right hand side with the railway visible from the road; From the South: Take the Evesham bypass then follow the B4088 to Dunnington.

BAGGERIDGE MINIATURE RAILWAY

Address: Baggeridge Country Park, Near Sedgley, Staffordshire   DY3 4HB
Telephone Nº: (01922) 476373
Year Formed: 1986
Location: Baggeridge Country Park
Length: Ground level line is being extended to 2,100 feet. Raised track is 420 feet

Nº of Steam Locos: 15
Nº of Other Locos: 7
Approx Nº of Visitors P.A.: Not known
Gauge: 3½ inches, 5 inches & 7¼ inches
Website: www.wolverhampton-dmes.co.uk

GENERAL INFORMATION

Nearest Mainline Station: Wolverhampton (7 miles)
Nearest Bus Station: Sedgley (2 miles)
Car Parking: Available on site
Coach Parking: Available on site
Food & Drinks: Available

SPECIAL INFORMATION

The Wolverhampton & District Model Engineering Society operates the railway which runs through the Baggeridge Country Park. This was formerly the Baggeridge Colliery and part of the original Himley Estate of the Earls of Dudley. Since the closure of the Colliery, the site has been transformed into 150 acres of attractive country park.

OPERATING INFORMATION

Opening Times: 2024 dates: Public running commences on 23rd March and the railway then operates on all Bank Holidays and most Sundays until 22nd September and also on 27th October & 24th November. Detailed information is available on the website. Trains run from 1.00pm to 4.00pm, weather permitting.
Steam Working: Most operating days.
Prices: No charge but donations are welcomed.

Detailed Directions by Car:
Take the A449 Wolverhampton to Kidderminster road then turn onto the A463 towards Sedgley. Baggeridge Country Park is just to the South of the A463 after approximately 1 mile and is well-signposted from the road.

BARNARDS MINIATURE RAILWAY

Address: Barnards Farm, Brentwood Road, West Horndon   CM13 3FY
Telephone Nº: (01277) 811262
Year Formed: 2010
Web: www.barnardsminiaturerailway.eu
E-mail: bmr@barnardsminiaturerailway.eu

Location: Off the A128 between Basildon & Hornchurch
Length of Line: Almost 1 mile
Nº of Steam Locos: 9   **Other Locos:** 6
Approx Nº of Visitors P.A.: 3,000
Gauge: 7¼ inches

GENERAL INFORMATION

Nearest Mainline Station: West Horndon (1½ miles)
Car Parking: Available on site
Coach Parking: Available on site
Food & Drinks: Available on site

SPECIAL INFORMATION

The Railway is located at Barnards Farm and runs through 17 hectares of gardens which range from landscaped walks through young woodland to the precise detail of the Japanese garden. A significant collection of sculpture by artists of many nationalities is also spread throughout the gardens. The gardens are open to the public on certain days during the year and visitors to the railway will need to pay an additional entrance fee on these days. Please check www.barnardsfarm.eu for further information.

OPERATING INFORMATION

Opening Times: 2024 dates: 30th & 31st March; 4th, 11th, 14th & 28th April; 12th, 26th & 30th May; 9th, 23rd & 30th June; 7th, 18th, 20th, 21st & 25th July; 1st, 4th, 8th, 15th, 22nd & 29th August; 1st, 4th, 8th, 15th, 18th, 22nd & 29th August; 1st, 15th, 28th & 29th September; 13th & 27th October; 8th, 9th, 10th & 30th November; 1st, 7th & 8th December.
Steam Working: Please contact the railway for further information.
Prices: Return £7.00
(Under-3s ride free)
All Day Travel Ticket £10.00
Note: Advance bookings are required for the Santa Specials in December.

Detailed Directions by Car:
From the West: Exit the M25 at Junction 29 and head eastward on the A127. After approximately 6½ miles exit onto the A128 and follow the road towards Tilbury. Turn right into the Barnard Farm car park shortly after passing under the railway line; From the East: Follow the A127 westward from Basildon and exit onto the A128 towards Tilbury. Then as above.

BARTON HOUSE RAILWAY

Address: Hartwell Road, The Avenue, Wroxham   NR12 8TL
Telephone Nº: (01603) 782008
Year Formed: 1963
Location of Line: Wroxham, Norfolk
Length of Line: 167 yards

Nº of Steam Locos: 4
Nº of Other Locos: 4
Approx Nº of Visitors P.A.: 1,250
Gauge: 3½ inches and 7¼ inches
Website: www.bhrw.org.uk

GENERAL INFO

Nearest Mainline Station:
Hoveton and Wroxham (1 mile)
Nearest Bus Station:
Wroxham (1 mile)
Car Parking: Limited parking available on site
Coach Parking: None
Souvenir Shop(s): Yes
Food & Drinks: Available

SPECIAL INFO

The original Honing East signalbox was rebuilt at Wroxham to form the basis for the Barton House Railway which is run entirely by volunteers. On open days, a boat service operates from Wroxham Bridge to take passengers to the railway.

OPERATING INFO

Opening Times: 2024 dates: 1st April then the 3rd Sunday each month from April until October. Trains run from 2.30pm to 5.30pm. Also open on the 3rd Saturday in September from 7.00pm to 10.00pm.
Steam Working:
Most operating days.
Prices: Adults £5.00 (£10.00)
            Children £2.50 (£5.00)
Note: On open days, access to the railway is also available via an electric launch service running from Wroxham Bridge. Prices in brackets for unlimited rides.

Detailed Directions by Car:
From the South and West: Take the A1151 from Norwich to Wroxham then follow the road over the railway bridge. Take the 3rd turning on the right into 'The Avenue', first left into Staitheway Road then right into Hartwell Road. The railway is at the end of the road; From the North: Take the A149 to the A1151 to Wroxham, turn left into 'The Avenue', then as above.

BATH & WEST RAILWAY

Address: The Royal Bath and West Showground, Shepton Mallet BA4 6QN
Year Formed: 2001
Length of Line: ½ mile
Nº of Steam Locos: 11
Nº of Other Locos: 3

Approx Nº of Visitors P.A.: 11,000
Gauge: 5 inches and 7¼ inches
Website: www.essmee.org.uk
E-mail: chair@essmee.org.uk

GENERAL INFORMATION

Nearest Mainline Station: Castle Cary (4 miles)
Nearest Bus Station: Shepton Mallet
Car Parking: Free parking available on site
Coach Parking: Available
Food & Drinks: Available during shows

SPECIAL INFORMATION

The Bath & West Railway is operated by members of the East Somerset Society of Model and Experimental Engineers Ltd.

OPERATING INFORMATION

Opening Times: The railway is situated on The Royal Bath & West Showground, Shepton Mallet. Our operating days, as well as our ability to entertain visitors with their locos, are therefore governed by which particular shows are using the showground. The railway operates on the three days of the Royal Bath & West Show from 30th May to 1st June 2024. Agreements between the Society and other shows may mean that the railway also operates on other dates during 2024. Please check the Society's website for public running dates in 2024 before visiting. The Society has an open weekend planned for 22nd to 24th April and other dates will be shown on the website.
Steam Working: All public operating days.
Prices: £2.00 per ride. Also 6 rides for £10.00 or 10 rides for £15.00
Note: An entrance fee is charged by the show organisers for their events.

Detailed Directions by Car:
From All Parts: The Royal Bath and West Showground is situated approximately 2 miles south of Shepton Mallet just off the A371 road to Castle Cary.

BEER HEIGHTS LIGHT RAILWAY

Address: Pecorama, Beer, East Devon, EX12 3NA	**N° of Steam Locos:** 8 at present
Telephone N°: (01297) 21542	**N° of Other Locos:** 3
Year Formed: 1975	**Approx N° of Visitors P.A.:** 80,000
Location of Line: Beer, East Devon	**Gauge:** 7¼ inches
Length of Line: 1 mile	**Website:** www.pecorama.co.uk
	E-mail: info@pecobeer.co.uk

GENERAL INFORMATION

Nearest Mainline Station: Axminster
Nearest Bus Stop: Beer
Car Parking: Available on site
Coach Parking: Available on site
Souvenir Shop(s): Yes
Food & Drinks: Licensed restaurant on site

SPECIAL INFORMATION

In addition to the Railway, Pecorama features a Model Railway Exhibition, childrens activity areas and extensive gardens.

OPERATING INFORMATION

Opening Times: 2024 dates: Daily from 26th March to 3rd November.
Steam Working: On every operating day, weather permitting.
Prices: Adult £14.50
Child £12.50 (Under-3s free of charge)
Concessions £12.50
Family Tickets £49.95 to £59.95
The prices shown above include entry to the Gardens, one ride on the railway and entry to the Model Railway Exhibition.

Detailed Directions by Car:
From All Parts: Take the A3052 to Beer, turn onto the B3174 and follow the Brown Tourist signs for Pecorama.

BEKONSCOT LIGHT RAILWAY

Address: Bekonscot Model Village & Railway, Warwick Road, Beaconsfield, Bucks   HP9 2PL
Telephone Nº: (01494) 672919
Year Formed: 2001 (Originally 1929)
Location of Line: Beaconsfield, Bucks.
Length of Line: 400 yards

Nº of Steam Locos: None at present
Nº of Other Locos: 3
Approx Nº of Visitors P.A.: 180,000
Gauge: 7¼ inches
Website: www.bekonscot.co.uk
Email: info@bekonscot.co.uk

GENERAL INFORMATION

Nearest Mainline Station: Beaconsfield (5 minutes walk)
Nearest Bus Station: High Wycombe
Car Parking: Limited spaces adjacent to the site
Coach Parking: Limited spaces adjacent to the site
Souvenir Shop(s): Yes
Food & Drinks: Available

SPECIAL INFORMATION

The Railway is situated in Bekonscot Model Village, a 1½ acre miniature landscape of fields, farms, castles, churches, woods and lakes which also contains a model railway.

OPERATING INFORMATION

Opening Times: 2024 dates: Daily from 2nd March to 3rd November. Open 10.00am to 5.30pm.
Steam Working: None at present
Prices: Adult £13.20
　　　　　　Child £8.40 (Ages 2–15 years)
　　　　　　Family Tickets £26.40 and £37.00
　　　　　　Concessions £12.80

Note: Prices shown above are for entrance into Bekonscot Model Village which is required to visit the railway. Visitors are urged to voluntarily pay higher prices so Gift aid can be claimed. Reduced rates are available for groups of 15 or more.

Detailed Directions by Car:
From All Parts: Exit the M40 at Junction 2 taking the A355 then follow the signs for the "Model Village".

BENTLEY MINIATURE RAILWAY

Address: Bentley, Harveys Lane, Ringmer   BN8 5AF
Telephone Nº: 0845 867-2583
Year Formed: 1985
Location of Line: 5 miles North of Lewes
Length of Line: 1 mile

Nº of Steam Locos: Members locos only
Nº of Other Locos: Members locos only
Approx Nº of Visitors P.A.: 10,000
Gauge: 7¼ inches
Website: www.bentleyrailway.co.uk
E-mail: enquiries@bentleyrailway.co.uk

GENERAL INFORMATION

Nearest Mainline Station: Uckfield (4 miles)
Nearest Bus Station: Uckfield (4 miles)
Car Parking: Free parking available on site
Coach Parking: Free parking available on site
Souvenir Shop(s): None
Food & Drinks: None

SPECIAL INFORMATION

The railway is owned and operated by volunteer members of the Bentley Miniature Railway Ltd and operates a wide variety of locomotives.

OPERATING INFORMATION

Opening Times: 2024 dates: Weekends and Bank Holidays from 29th March to 29th September and Wednesdays during the East Sussex school holidays. Santa Specials run on selected days in December. Trains run from 11.30am to 4.00pm (but 11.00am to 5.00pm during the summer).
Steam Working: Most Sundays.
Prices: £2.00 per ride
Unlimited Ride tickets £5.00 per person

Detailed Directions by Car:
From All Parts: Bentley Wildfowl & Motor Museum is located just outside of the village of Shortgate by the B2192 road between Halland (which located by at the junction of the B2192 and A22) and Lewes (A26/A27). The Museum is well-signposted locally from the A22 (Uckfield to Eastbourne), A26 (Uckfield to Lewes) and B2192.

Bromsgrove Society of Model Engineers

Address: Avoncroft Museum of Historic Buildings, Stoke Heath, Bromsgrove, B60 4JR
Year Formed: 1980s
Location: In the grounds of the museum
Length of Line: 1,260 feet

Nº of Steam Locos: Members locos only
Nº of Other Locos: 4 + members locos
Approx Nº of Visitors P.A.: Not known
Gauge: 2½ inches, 3½ inches, 5 inches and smaller gauges
Website: www.bromsgrovesme.co.uk

GENERAL INFORMATION

Nearest Mainline Station: Bromsgrove (1.5 miles)
Nearest Bus Station: Stoke Heath
Car Parking: In the Museum car park
Coach Parking: Available
Souvenir Shop(s): In the Museum only
Food & Drinks: Available

OPERATING INFORMATION

Opening Times: 2024 dates: 10th & 29th March; 1st, 20th & 21st April; 5th, 6th &27th May; 15th & 16th June; 24th & 31st July; 7th, 14th, 16th, 21st, 25th & 31st July; 7th, 14th, 16th, 21st, 25th & 26th September; 12th & 13th October.
Trains run from 10.30am to 5.00pm.
Steam Working: Most operating days
Prices: Adults £14.00
   Children £6.50 (Under-5s free)
   Students £9.90
   Families £26.00 to £38.00
Note: Prices shown are for entrance into the Museum. Train rides are an additional £1.00 per person.

Detailed Directions by Car:
The track site is adjacent to Avoncroft Museum of Historic Buildings which is situated just off the A38 Bromsgrove bypass. From the South: The Museum is signposted from Junction 5 of the M5; From the North: The Museum is signposted from Junction 1 of the M42. After turning off the road into the museum, the club's private entrance gates are to the left of Avoncroft's main entrance. SatNav users should use B60 4JR as the destination post code.

BROOKSIDE MINIATURE RAILWAY

Address: London Road North (A523), Poynton, Cheshire SK12 1BY
Telephone Nº: 0781 807-0723
Year Formed: 1989
Location: Brookside Garden Centre
Length of Line: Almost ¾ mile

Nº of Steam Locos: Visiting locos only
Nº of Other Locos: 3
Approx Nº of Visitors P.A.: 70,000
Gauge: 7¼ inches

GENERAL INFORMATION

Nearest Mainline Station: Poynton and Hazel Grove (both 1 mile)
Nearest Bus Station: Stockport (5 miles).
Car Parking: 300 spaces available on site
Coach Parking: 2 spaces available
Souvenir Shop(s): Yes
Food & Drinks: Yes

SPECIAL INFORMATION

The Railway runs through the grounds of the Brookside Garden Centre. There is also an extensive collection of Railwayana on display.

OPERATING INFORMATION

Opening Times: The Railway is open Thursdays to Sundays and Bank Holidays.
Trains usually run from 10.45am to 4.00pm.
Steam Working: No set dates as it is dependent on visiting locos.
Prices: Adult £2.50 per ride
(buy 10 tickets and get 2 extra rides free)

Detailed Directions by Car:
From the North: Exit the M60 at Junction 1 in Stockport and take the A6 (signposted Buxton). Upon reaching Hazel Grove, take the A523 to Poynton. Follow the brown tourist signs for the Railway; From the West: Exit the M56 at Junction 6 signposted Wilmslow and continue to Poynton. Follow the brown signs for the Railway; From the South: Exit the M6 at Junction 18 for Holmes Chapel. Follow the signs to Wilmslow, then as from the West; From the East: Follow the A6 to Hazel Grove, then as from the North.

BROOMY HILL RAILWAY

Address: Broomy Hill, Hereford	**Nº of Steam Locos:** 4+
Telephone Nº: 07763 897678	**Nº of Other Locos:** 2+
Year Formed: 1962	**Approx Nº of Visitors P.A.:** Not known
Location of Line: Adjacent to the	**Gauge:** 7¼ inches, 5 inches, 3½ inches
Waterworks Museum, Hereford	**Website:** www.hsme.co.uk
Length of Line: Approximately 1 mile	**E-mail:** secretary@hsme.co.uk

GENERAL INFORMATION

Nearest Mainline Station: Hereford (1½ miles)
Nearest Bus Station: Hereford (1½ miles)
Car Parking: Free parking available on site
Coach Parking: Available by prior arrangement
Souvenir Shop(s): Yes
Food & Drinks: Available

SPECIAL INFORMATION

The Broomy Hill Railway is operated by the
Hereford Society of Model Engineers and has two
separate tracks which run along the bank of the
River Wye. Members run their own locomotives so
the number and variety in operation may vary from
day to day. Entry to the site is free of charge and
picnic areas are available.

OPERATING INFORMATION

Opening Times: 2024 dates: 21st April;
12th, 26th & 27th May; 9th & 30th June;
14th & 28th July; 11th, 25th & 26th August;
8th & 29th September; 13th & 26th October.
Trains run from 12.00pm to 4.30pm (2.00pm to
6.00pm for the Halloween trains on 26th October).
Steam Working: All operating days.
Prices: Adults £1.50 per ride
                  Children £1.50 per ride
Note: Four rides can be bought for £5.00 and
children's parties can be arranged. Also, the site is
prone to flooding so open days may sometimes be
cancelled following heavy rainfall!

Detailed Directions by Car:
From the centre of Hereford, take the A49 Ross-on-Wye Road, turning right into Barton Road. After approximately
400 metres, turn left into Broomy Hill Road, proceed for around 600 metres before turning left following signs
for the Waterworks Museum. The railway is on the right just after the museum which is signposted with Brown
Tourist Information Signs.

CAMBRIDGE & DISTRICT MODEL ENGINEERING SOCIETY

Address: Fulbrooke Road, Cambridge, CB3 9EE	**Nº of Steam Locos:** 12
Telephone Nº: none	**Nº of Other Locos:** 4
Year Formed: 1938	**Approx Nº of Visitors P.A.:** 3,500
Location of Line: Newnham, Cambridge	**Gauge:** 3½ inches, 5 inches and 7¼ inches
Length of Line: ¾ mile	**Website:** www.cdmes.uk

GENERAL INFORMATION

Nearest Mainline Station: Cambridge (2 miles)
Nearest Bus Station: Drummer Street (1 mile)
Car Parking: Available on site (no street parking)
Coach Parking: None
Souvenir Shop(s): None
Food & Drinks: Cafe open on operating days

SPECIAL INFORMATION

The Cambridge & District MES was formed in 1938 and the track and clubhouse in Fulbrooke Road was constructed on a 2 acre site during 1959.

OPERATING INFORMATION

Opening Times: 2024 dates: 14th April; 12th May; 9th June; 14th July; 11th August; 8th September; 13th October. Gates open at 12.30pm and trains operate from 1.30pm to 5.30pm.
Steam Working: Every operating day.
Prices: Adults £2.50 (5 rides for £10.00)
Note: Under-5s must be accompanied by an adult and Under-3s ride free of charge.

Detailed Directions by Car:
The Railway is located in the south-western part of Cambridge in the suburb of Newnham, just behind the ground of Cambridge Rugby Club. Exit the M11 at Junction 12 and follow the A603 (Barton Road) into Cambridge. After approximately 1½ miles, turn right into Grantchester Road. Car parking for the railway is signposted from Grantchester Road and is normally at the Rugby Club itself.

CANVEY MINIATURE RAILWAY

Address: Waterside Farm Sports Centre, Somnes Avenue, Canvey Island   SS8 9RA
Year Formed: 1976
Location of Line: Canvey Island
Length of Line: Two lines, one of 1,440 feet and one of 4,400 feet (7¼ inch line)

Nº of Steam Locos: Variable
Nº of Other Locos: Variable
Approx Nº of Visitors P.A.: 6,000
Gauge: 3½ inches, 5 inches & 7¼ inches
Website: www.cramec.org

GENERAL INFORMATION

Nearest Mainline Station: Benfleet (1 mile)
Nearest Bus Station: Bus stop just outside
Car Parking: Available on site
Coach Parking: Available on site
Food & Drinks: None

SPECIAL INFORMATION

The railway is operated by members of the Canvey Railway and Model Engineering Club.

OPERATING INFORMATION

Opening Times: 2024 dates: Every Sunday from 24th March until 13th October. Also open for Santa Specials on 1st and 8th December. Please contact the railway for further information. Trains run from 10.30am to 3.45pm, weather permitting.
Steam Working: When available on operating days.
Prices: £2.00 per ride.
Note: Higher prices apply for Santa Specials.

Detailed Directions by Car:
All road routes to Canvey Island meet at the Waterside Farm roundabout. The railway lines are located in the grounds of the Sports Complex/Leisure Centre. Turn right at the traffic lights into the centre and the car park is on the left with the railway on the right.

CHELMSFORD SOCIETY OF MODEL ENGINEERS

Address: Meteor Way (off Waterhouse Lane), Chelmsford, Essex CM1 2RL
Telephone Nº: None
Year Formed: 1935
Location of Line: Chelmsford
Length of Line: Two tracks, each approximately 1,000 feet long
Web site: www.chelmsfordsocietyofmodelengineers.org.uk

Nº of Steam Locos: 40+ (owned by
Nº of Other Locos: 20+   members)
Approx Nº of Visitors P.A.: 1,500
Gauge: 3½ inches, 5 inches & 7¼ inches
E-mail: webmaster@csme.org.uk

GENERAL INFORMATION

Nearest Mainline Station: Chelmsford (½ mile)
Nearest Bus Station: Chelmsford (½ mile)
Car Parking: Available adjacent to the railway (currently free of charge at weekends)
Food & Drinks: Light refreshments available

SPECIAL INFORMATION

The Chelmsford Society of Model Engineers promotes the safe construction and operation of passenger-carrying steam, electric and diesel hauled trains, traction engines and other scale models.

OPERATING INFORMATION

Opening Times: 2024 dates: Every Sunday from 28th April to 6th October inclusive. Santa Specials operate in December. Trains usually run from 2.00pm to 4.30pm on running dates.
A number of Special Events are held during the year. Please check the Society's website for further details.
Steam Working: Most operating days.
Prices: £1.50 per ride or £5.00 for 6 rides.

Detailed Directions by Car:
From London: Follow the A12 then take the A1016 towards Chelmsford town centre. Continue past the A414 junctions into Westway then into Waterhouse Lane. Meteor Way is on the right after the fourth set of traffic lights, just before the river. Park and then proceed past the five bar gate to the club entrance on the right; From Southend: Follow the A130 to the A12 junction then cross onto the A1114. After 1¼ miles join the A414 towards Chelmsford. Follow the A414 around Chelmsford to the junction with the A1016 at Widford. Take the 2nd exit into Westway then as from London; From Colchester: Follow the A12 and exit at the A414 junction towards Chelmsford. Follow the A414 to the A1016, then as from Southend.

CHESTERFIELD & DISTRICT M.E.S.

Address: The Clubhouse, Hady Hill, Bolsover Road, Chesterfield S41 0EE
Telephone Nº: None
Year Formed: 1932
Location of Line: In the grounds of St. Peter & St. Paul School, Chesterfield
Length of Line: Two lines – one of 1,100 feet and one of 2,500 feet

Nº of Steam Locos: 1 + members engines
Nº of Other Locos: 3 + members engines
Approx Nº of Visitors P.A.: 5,000
Gauge: 2½ inches, 3½ inches, 5 inches and 7¼ inches
Website: www.cdmes.co.uk
E-mail: enquiries@cdmes.co.uk

GENERAL INFORMATION

Nearest Mainline Station: Chesterfield (1½ miles)
Nearest Bus Station: Chesterfield (1 mile)
Car Parking: Available on site
Coach Parking: Available by prior arrangement
Food & Drinks: Available

SPECIAL INFORMATION

There are excellent facilities at Hady including tracks for locomotives and, as the land is undulating, both the ground level and raised tracks make challenging driving for all locomotives. The Society also owns the track, locomotive and running stock at Papplewick Pumping Station, Ravenshead, Notts where events are also run on behalf of The Papplewick Association.

OPERATING INFORMATION

Opening Times: 2024 dates: Public running days at Hady are 25th & 26th May and 7th & 8th September. Santa Specials operate in December but the operating days are not decided until later in the year when pre-bookings are essential so please check the website for updates
Steam Working: All operational days.
Prices: Admission is free. Rides are £2.00 per person per ride.

Detailed Directions by Car:
The Society is located on the top of Hady Hill, two-thirds of a mile from the town on Bolsover Road, A632. Driving out of Chesterfield, as you get to the top of the steep hill, turn left off the main road into the grounds of St. Peter & St. Paul School. Follow the drive around to the left and then take the first right. The site is at the end of the drive, after about 250 yards.

CHINGFORD & DISTRICT M.E.C.

Address: Ridgeway Park, Peel Close, Old Church Road, Chingford E4 6XU
Telephone N°: None
Year Formed: 1945
Location: Ridgeway Park, Chingford
Length of Lines: 1,000 feet (5 inch track) and 3,000 feet (7¼ inch track)
Website: www.chingford-model-engineering.com
E-mail: secretary@chingford-model-engineering.com

N° of Steam Locos: 11 (owned by Club)
N° of Other Locos: Many
Approx N° of Visitors P.A.: 17,000
Gauge: 3½ inches, 5 inches & 7¼ inches

GENERAL INFORMATION

Nearest Mainline Station: Chingford (1½ miles)
Nearest Underground Station: Walthamstow Central (5 miles)
Car Parking: Limited spaces within the Park
Coach Parking: None
Food & Drinks: None

SPECIAL INFORMATION

The Chingford & District Model Engineering Club seeks to promote all forms of model engineering and model making. It's members come from all walks of life, and do not necessarily have an engineering background.

OPERATING INFORMATION

Opening Times: 2024 dates: Sundays and Bank Holidays from 7th April to 6th October inclusive and also on Wednesdays during August.
Train rides usually run from 2.00pm to 5.30pm.
Steam Working: Practically every operating day.
Prices: £1.00 per person per ride on the raised track
£2.00 per person per ride on the ground track
Note: The Railway is available to hire for children's parties during the summer months.

Detailed Directions by Car:
Ridgeway Park is situated off the A112 Old Church Road in Chingford. Turn into Peel Close and the Park entrance is on the left after 50 yards at the mini-roundabout. A small car park is situated in Ridgeway Park. The railway itself is located about 150 yards down the main path on the right.

CROWBOROUGH MINIATURE RAILWAY

Address: Goldsmiths Leisure Centre, Eridge Road, Crowborough TN6 2TN
Telephone Nº: (01892) 852741
Year Formed: 1990
Location of Line: Crowborough
Length of Line: 1,000 feet
Website: www.crowboroughminiaturerailway.com

Nº of Steam Locos: Members locos only
Nº of Other Locos: 1
Approx Nº of Visitors P.A.: 1,500
Gauge: 3½ inches, 5 inches & 7¼ inches

GENERAL INFORMATION

Nearest Mainline Station: Crowborough (1½ miles)
Nearest Bus Station: Tunbridge Wells (7 miles)
Car Parking: Available on site
Coach Parking: Available on site
Food & Drinks: Available at the Leisure Centre

SPECIAL INFORMATION

The Crowborough Locomotive Society was formed to build, maintain, and run a miniature railway at the Leisure Centre in Crowborough. The society runs live steam working locomotives to give both young and old alike a railway journey in miniature!

OPERATING INFORMATION

Opening Times: 2024 dates: Saturday afternoons and Bank Holidays from 30th March until 2nd November. A Special Bonfire Night event is held on 5th November and Santa Specials run on 14th & 26th December. Trains run from 2.00pm to 5.00pm.
Steam Working: Most operational days, depending on which members' locos are running.
Prices: £1.00 for one circuit of the extended track Day Rover tickets are £4.00
Note: Birthday parties can be held at the railway by prior arrangement.

Detailed Directions by Car:
Goldsmiths Leisure Centre is situated in the north of Crowborough just off the A26 (Eridge Road) which is the main Tunbridge Wells to Uckfield through road.

CUTTESLOWE PARK MINIATURE RAILWAY

Address: Cutteslowe Park, Harbord Road, Oxford   OX2 8NB
(SatNav OX2 8LH – House Number 41!)
Year Formed: 1955
Location: Cutteslowe Park, Oxford
Length of Line: Two lines – 390 yard raised line and 500 yard ground level line

Nº of Steam Locos: 40
Nº of Other Locos: 15
Approx Nº of Visitors P.A.: 30,000
Gauge: 3½ inches, 5 inches & 7¼ inches

GENERAL INFORMATION

Nearest Mainline Station: Oxford (3¼ miles)
Nearest Bus Station: Oxford (3 miles)
Car Parking: Available on site
Coach Parking: Available by prior arrangement
Food & Drinks: Refreshments are available in Cutteslowe Park

SPECIAL INFORMATION

The Cutteslowe Park Miniature Railway is operated by the City of Oxford Society of Model Engineers.

OPERATING INFORMATION

Opening Times: 2024 dates: The 1st, 3rd and occasional 5th Sunday from 31st March to 27th October inclusive. Also open on Bank Holidays from April to the end of October and on Wednesday afternoons during the summer holidays. Trains run from 1.30pm to 5.00pm (4.30pm in October).
Steam Working: Up to 5 steam locomotives run on every operating day.
Prices: £1.50 per ride (Under-2s ride free)
             10 rides are available for £12.50

Detailed Directions by Car:
From outside of Oxford join the ringroad and head to the North of the city. At the roundabout at the junction of the A40 ringroad and the A4165 Banbury Road, head North signposted for Kidlington. Take the third turn on the right into Harbord Road which leads directly into the Park. Follow the signs from the car park for the Railway.

DEVON RAILWAY CENTRE

Address: The Station, Bickleigh,
Tiverton   EX16 8RG
Telephone Nº: (01884) 855671
Year Formed: 1997
Location of Line: Bickleigh, Devon
Length of Line: ½ mile (2 foot and 7¼ inch
gauges); 200 yards (Standard gauge)

Nº of Steam Locos: 1
Nº of Other Locos: 12
Approx Nº of Visitors P.A.: Not recorded
Gauge: 2 feet, 7¼ inches and Standard
Website: www.devonrailwaycentre.co.uk
E-mail: devonrailway@btinternet.com

GENERAL INFORMATION

Nearest Mainline Station: Exeter
Nearest Bus Station: Tiverton (Route 55)
Car Parking: Available on site
Coach Parking: Available on site
Souvenir Shop(s): Yes
Food & Drinks: Yes

SPECIAL INFORMATION

Devon Railway Centre has passenger-carrying lines
and also features a large model railway exhibition
with 15 working layouts. A delightful Edwardian
model village built to a 1:12 scale has recently been
extended with a model funfair added and a new
museum coach is also available.

OPERATING INFORMATION

Opening Times: 2024 dates: Daily from 29th
March to 14th April, then all weekends from 20th
April to 3rd October. Also open on Thursdays and
Fridays from 2nd May to 29th September and
Tuesdays and Wednesdays in July and August.
Open from 10.30am until 5.00pm on all operating
days.
Steam Working: Please check the website for details.
Prices: Adult £12.80   Child £11.80
            Senior Citizen £12.30
            Family £47.90-£58.00 (Under-3s free)
Admission includes unlimited train rides and access
to the model village, model railways, museum and
crazy golf.

Detailed Directions by Car:
From All Parts: Devon Railway Centre is situated adjacent to the famous Bickleigh Bridge, just off the A396
Exeter to Tiverton road (3 miles from Tiverton and 8 miles from Exeter).

DRAGON MINIATURE RAILWAY

Address: Dobbies Garden Centre, Dooley Lane, Marple, Stockport, SK6 7HE
Telephone Nº: 07748 581160
Year Formed: 1999
Location of Line: Marple Garden Centre
Length of Line: ½ mile

Nº of Steam Locos: 10
Nº of Other Locos: 6
Approx Nº of Visitors P.A.: 30,000
Gauge: 7¼ inches
Web: www.dragonrailway2023.wixsite.com
E-mail: dragonrailway@hotmail.co.uk

GENERAL INFORMATION

Nearest Mainline Station: Romley (1 mile)
Nearest Bus Station: Stockport (2½ miles)
Car Parking: Available on site
Coach Parking: Available
Souvenir Shop(s): Yes
Food & Drinks: Available

SPECIAL INFORMATION

Dragon Miniature Railway is one of the few Garden Centre-based railways which operates steam on most open days.

OPERATING INFORMATION

Opening Times: Weekends and Bank Holidays and also daily during local school holidays throughout the year. Trains run from 11.00am to 4.30pm, weather permitting.
Steam Working: Most operating days.
Prices: £1.50 per ride (Under-2s free of charge)
Ten-ride tickets are available for £12.00

Detailed Directions by Car:
From All Parts: Exit the M60 at Junction 25, pass through Bredbury and follow signs for Marple along the A627. Cross over the River Goyt and Marple Garden Centre is on the left.

EASTBOURNE MINIATURE STEAM RAILWAY

Address: E.M.S.R. Adventure Park, Lottbridge Drove, Eastbourne, East Sussex BN23 6QJ
Telephone Nº: (01323) 520229
Year Formed: 1992
Location of Line: Eastbourne

Length of Line: 1 mile
Nº of Steam Locos: 7
Nº of Other Locos: 3
Approx Nº of Visitors P.A.: Not known
Gauge: 7¼ inches
Website: www.emsr.co.uk

GENERAL INFORMATION

Nearest Mainline Station: Eastbourne (2 miles)
Nearest Bus Station: Eastbourne (2 miles)
Car Parking: Free parking on site
Coach Parking: Free parking on site
Souvenir Shop(s): Yes
Food & Drinks: Yes

SPECIAL INFORMATION

The Railway site also has many other attractions including model railways, an adventure playground, maze, nature walk, picnic area and a Cafe.

OPERATING INFORMATION

Opening Times: 2024 dates: Daily from 6th April until 3rd November. Trains run from 10.00am to 5.00pm during these days.
Steam Working: Weekends, Bank Holidays and during School Holidays. Diesel at other times.
Prices: Adult £12.00
　　　　　Child £12.00 (Under-3s ride free)
　　　　　Concessions £10.50 to £11.00
Entry to the Park includes one ride but extra rides cost £1.50 each.

Detailed Directions by Car:
From All Parts: Take the A22 new road to Eastbourne then follow the Brown tourist signs for the 'Mini Railway'.

EAST HERTS MINIATURE RAILWAY

Address: Van Hage Garden Centre,
Great Amwell, near Ware   SG12 9RP
Telephone Nº: (020) 8292-2997
Year Formed: 1978
Location: Van Hage Garden Centre
Length of Line: 500 metres

Nº of Steam Locos: 4
Nº of Other Locos: 4
Approx Nº of Visitors P.A.: 40,000
Gauge: 7¼ inches
Website: www.ehmr.org.uk

GENERAL INFORMATION

Nearest Mainline Station: Ware (1½ miles)
Nearest Bus Station: Bus stop outside the Centre
Car Parking: Available on site
Coach Parking: Available
Food & Drinks: Available in the Garden Centre

SPECIAL INFORMATION

The Railway operates a line at the Van Hage Garden Centre in Great Amwell. The railway is run by volunteers and any profits are donated to the local special needs school and other local charities.

OPERATING INFORMATION

Opening Times: Weekends and Bank Holidays throughout the year. Also open Tuesdays and Thursdays during the school holidays. Usually open from 11.00am to 5.00pm but from 10.30am to 4.30pm on Sundays.
Steam Working: Most operating days.
Prices: £1.50 per person per ride. Under-2s travel free of charge and Under-8s must be accompanied by an older, fare-paying passenger.

Detailed Directions by Car:
From the South: Take the A10 towards Cambridge and exit at the first Ware junction signposted for A414. Take the 2nd exit at the roundabout onto the A1170 towards Ware and Van Hage Garden Centre is on the left after 600 metres; From the East: Take the A414 from Harlow and turn off onto the A1170 for Ware. Then as above.

EATON PARK MINIATURE RAILWAY

Address: Eaton Park, Colman Road, Norwich NR4 7AU	**N⁰ of Steam Locos:** 2 + visiting locos
Year Formed: 1933	**N⁰ of Other Locos:** 2
Location of Line: Eaton Park, Norwich	**Approx N⁰ of Visitors P.A.:** 16,000
Length of Line: Two tracks – 'Mainline' is 800 metres (7¼ and 5 inch gauges) and the 'Heritage Track' is 955 feet (raised 5 and 3½ inch gauges)	**Gauge:** 3½ inches, 5 inches & 7¼ inches

Address: Eaton Park, Colman Road, Norwich NR4 7AU
Year Formed: 1933
Location of Line: Eaton Park, Norwich
Length of Line: Two tracks – 'Mainline' is 800 metres (7¼ and 5 inch gauges) and the 'Heritage Track' is 955 feet (raised 5 and 3½ inch gauges)

N⁰ of Steam Locos: 2 + visiting locos
N⁰ of Other Locos: 2
Approx N⁰ of Visitors P.A.: 16,000
Gauge: 3½ inches, 5 inches & 7¼ inches
Website: www.ndsme.org
E-mail: epmrinfo@ndsme.org
Facebook: 'Eaton Park Miniature Railway'

GENERAL INFORMATION

Nearest Mainline Station: Norwich (3 miles)
Nearest Bus Station: Norwich (2 miles)
Car Parking: Available in Eaton Park
Coach Parking: None
Food & Drinks: Available in Eaton Park

SPECIAL INFORMATION

Norwich & District Society of Model Engineers was formed in 1933 and operates two tracks in Eaton Park. The 'Mainline' is a 7¼ inch and 5 inch ground level track and the 'Heritage Track' is a raised tracking using 5 inch and 3½ inch gauges.

OPERATING INFORMATION

Opening Times: 2024 dates: Sundays and Bank Holidays from 31st March to 6th October. Trains run from 1.00pm to 5.00pm, weather permitting.
Steam Working: Most operating days
Prices: Adult £1.50 (All day tickets £5.00)
Child £1.00 (All day tickets £4.00)

Detailed Directions by Car:
Take the A11 or A140 into Norwich and upon reaching the ring road, turn left. At the second set of traffic lights turn left into South Park Avenue and the entrance to Eaton Park is on the right hand side.
Alternative route: Take the A47 into Norwich and turn right at the ring road. At the 3rd set of traffic lights turn right into South Park Avenue.

EVERGREENS MINIATURE RAILWAY

Address: Dawn Bank, Keal Cotes, Lincolnshire   PE23 4AE
Telephone Nº: (01754) 830574 or (01205) 480703
Year Formed: 2002
Location: Keal Coates, just off the A16
Website: www.evergreensminiaturerailway.org
E-mail: evergreensminiaturerailway@gmail.com

Nº of Steam Locos: 10
Nº of Other Locos: 14
Approx Nº of Visitors P.A.: Not known
Gauge: 5 inches and 7¼ inches

GENERAL INFORMATION

Nearest Mainline Station: Boston (12 miles)
Nearest Bus Station: Spilsby (4 miles)
Car Parking: Available on site
Coach Parking: None
Food & Drinks: Available

SPECIAL INFORMATION

Originally based in Stickney, the Railway has relocated to a new site in Keal Cotes in 2018. The new site is a 4½ acre field which has been named Dawn Bank.

OPERATING INFORMATION

Opening Times: 2024 dates: 30th March; 27th April; 25th May; 29th June; 27th July; 31st August; 28th September; 26th October and Santa Specials on 30th November. Trains will also operate on Wednesdays during the Summer school holidays. Trains run from 11.00am to 4.00pm.
Steam Working: Most operating days.
Prices: Admission £5.00
           Families £18.00 (2 adults + 2 children
                    or 1 adult + 3 children)
Note: The prices shown include unlimited rides.

Detailed Directions by Car:
The railway is situated in Keal Cotes, on the A16 between Boston and Spilsby. Upon reaching Keal Cotes, turn into Fen Road opposite The Coach House pub. Continue along Fen Road to the East Fen Catchwater Drain bridge and turn right immediately after crossing the bridge. Dawn Bank is along this road.

FANCOTT MINIATURE RAILWAY

Address: Fancott Miniature Railway, Fancott, near Toddington, Bedfordshire
Telephone Nº: 07917 756237
Year Formed: 1996
Location of Line: The Fancott Pub, near Toddington, Bedfordshire
Length of Line: ¼ mile

Nº of Steam Locos: None
Nº of Other Locos: 3
Approx Nº of Visitors P.A.: 10,000
Gauge: 7¼ inches
Website: www.fancottrailway.tk
E-mail: thefmr@live.co.uk

GENERAL INFORMATION

Nearest Mainline Station: Harlington/Leagrave
Nearest Bus Station: Luton
Car Parking: 50 spaces available on site
Coach Parking: Available but no special space
Souvenir Shop(s): No
Food & Drinks: Pub/Restaurant on site

SPECIAL INFORMATION

The Railway runs through the grounds of The Fancott Pub, a winner of the Whitbread Family Pub of the Year award.

OPERATING INFORMATION

Opening Times: 2024 dates: Weekends, Bank Holidays and School Holidays (except Mondays) from April to the end of September.
Trains usually run from 1.00pm to 5.00pm.
Steam Working: Steam locos visit on a regular basis – please contact the railway for further details.
Prices: £2.00 per ride

Detailed Directions by Car:
From All Parts: Exit the M1 at Junction 12 and travel towards Toddington. After approximately 100 yards, take the B579 towards Chalton and Fancott. The Fancott pub is on the left after the second bend.

Faversham Miniature Railway

Address: Brogdale Farm, Brogdale Road, Faversham, Kent   ME13 8XZ
Telephone Nº: (01795) 474211
Year Formed: 1984
Location of Line: Faversham, Kent
Length of Line: Approximately 1¼ miles
Gauge: 9 inches

Nº of Steam Locos: 6
Nº of Other Locos: 11
Approx Nº of Visitors P.A.: 6,000+
Web: www.favershamminiaturerailway.co.uk

GENERAL INFORMATION

Nearest Mainline Station: Faversham (¾ mile)
Nearest Bus Station: None, but a regular bus service travels to Faversham from Canterbury
Car Parking: Available on site
Coach Parking: Available on site
Souvenir Shop(s): Various shops on site
Food & Drinks: Available

SPECIAL INFORMATION

Faversham Miniature Railway is the only 9 inch gauge railway in the UK which is open to the public.

OPERATING INFORMATION

Opening Times: Sundays and Bank Holiday weekends from March to October from 11.00am to 4.00pm. Also open for Santa Specials and other Special Events in December.
Please contact the railway for further information.
Steam Working: Special steam days only.
Please contact the Railway for further details.
Prices: £1.50 per ride
           £2.00 per ride when Steam-hauled
Note: Different prices may apply for Special Events.

Detailed Directions by Car:
Exit the M2 at Junction 5 and take the A251 towards Faversham. After about ½ mile turn left onto the A2 then left again after ¼ mile turning into Brogdale Road for the Farm and Railway.

FENLAND LIGHT RAILWAY

Address: Mereside Farm, Mereside Drove, Ramsey Mereside, Cambs.	**N° of Steam Locos:** 3+
Telephone N°: None	**N° of Other Locos:** 2+
Year Formed: 1991	**Approx N° of Visitors P.A.:** 500 – 1,000
Location of Line: Mereside Farm	**Gauge:** 7¼ inches
Length of Line: 800 feet	**Website:** www.fenlandlightrailway.co.uk

GENERAL INFORMATION

Nearest Mainline Station: Peterborough (10 miles)
Nearest Bus Station: Peterborough (10 miles)
Car Parking: Available on site
Coach Parking: None
Food & Drinks: Available

SPECIAL INFORMATION

The railway is operated by volunteers from the Ramsey Miniature Steam Railway Society. The Society undertakes running days at local school fetes, country fairs and charity events by prior arrangement using up to 600 feet of portable track.

OPERATING INFORMATION

Opening Times: The third Sunday of each month from March to November inclusive except for August when two days are spent at the nearby Ramsey Rural Museum Fair which was formerly held at RAF Upwood. Santa Special running days usually take place on dates during December (pre-booking required). Please check the railway's website for further information.
Steam Working: All operating days.
Prices: From £1.50 per ride
(visits and rides must be pre-booked)

Detailed Directions by Car:
From Ramsey: Travel up Great Whyte, turn right at the mini-roundabout by the Mill Apartments and follow onto Stocking Fen Road. Follow this road for just over a mile then turn left into Bodsey Toll Road for Ramsey Mereside. Follow this road until the signpost for Ramsey Mereside and turn right into Mereside Drove. The railway is on the left after approximately 1 mile.

FRIMLEY LODGE MINIATURE RAILWAY

Address: Frimley Lodge Park, Sturt Road, Frimley Green, Surrey   GU16 6HT
Phone Nº: 07710 606461 (Please use on operating days only)
Year Formed: 1991
Location of Line: Frimley Green
Length of Line: 1 kilometre

Nº of Steam Locos: 5 (Members' locos)
Nº of Other Locos: 3
Approx Nº of Visitors P.A.: 20,000+
Gauge: 3½ inches, 5 inches & 7¼ inches
Website: www.flmr.org

GENERAL INFORMATION

Nearest Mainline Station: Frimley or Ashvale (both 2 miles)
Nearest Bus Station: Farnborough (4 miles) – take the Number 3 bus between Aldershot and Yately.
Car Parking: Available on site
Coach Parking: Available by prior arrangement
Food & Drinks: Cafe in the Park

SPECIAL INFORMATION

The Railway is operated by volunteers from the Frimley and Ascot Locomotive Club who bring their own Locomotives to give pleasure to others. All the proceeds are used for the maintenance of the Railway and to benefit local charities.

OPERATING INFORMATION

Opening Times: 2024 dates: The first Sunday of the month from 3rd March to 3rd November. Also on some Wednesdays in the school holidays. Trains run from 11.00am to 5.00pm.
Santa Specials run on 8th December 11.00am to 2.30pm, but must be pre-booked.
Steam Working: Operational Sundays only.
Prices: Single Rides £1.50
　　　　　Family Ticket £12.00 (10 rides)

Detailed Directions by Car:
Exit the M3 at Junction 4 and take the A331 towards Guildford. Leave the A331 at the turn-off for Mytchett and turn left at the top of the ramp then left again at the Miners Arms into Sturt Road. Cross over the bridge then turn right into Frimley Lodge Park. Once in the Park turn right then right again then take the next left for the Railway.

GREAT COCKCROW RAILWAY

Address: Hardwick Lane, Lyne,
near Chertsey, Surrey   KT16 0AD
Telephone Nº: (01932) 565474 (Sundays)
Year Formed: 1968
Location of Line: Lyne, near Chertsey
Length of Line: 2 miles

Nº of Steam Locos: Approximately 25
Nº of Other Locos: 3
Approx Nº of Visitors P.A.: 10,000
Gauge: 7¼ inches
Website: www.cockcrow.co.uk

GENERAL INFORMATION

Nearest Mainline Station: Chertsey (30 min. walk)
Nearest Bus Stop: Chertsey (30 minute walk)
Car Parking: Available on site
Coach Parking: Limited parking available on site
Souvenir Shop(s): None
Food & Drinks: Available

SPECIAL INFORMATION

Emanating from the Greywood Central Railway, built from 1946, at a private address in Walton-on-Thames, the Great Cockcrow Railway opened in 1968 and has continually grown since moving to the present site. The Railway offers a choice of two regular routes, each served every few minutes.

OPERATING INFORMATION

Opening Times: 2024 dates: Sundays from 5th May to 27th October when trains run from 1.00pm to 4.30pm. Also open on Wednesdays in August (1.00pm to 4.00pm) and on Halloween Saturday 26th October (5.00pm to 8.00pm).
Steam Working: Every operating day
Prices: Adult Single £6.00
　　　　　Child Single £5.00
　　　　　Family Ticket £18.00

Detailed Directions by Car:
Exit the M25 at Junction 11 and take the A320 towards Woking. At the first roundabout take the exit towards Chertsey and continue along this road passing St. Peter's Hospital on the left, then turn next left (B386) towards Windlesham. Turn right almost immediately into Hardwick Lane and the railway on the right after about ¼ mile just after Hardwick Farm.　　Satellite Navigation: KT16 0AD

GRIMSBY & CLEETHORPES M.E.S.

Address: Waltham Windmill, Brigsley Road, Waltham, Grimsby   DN32 0JZ
Telephone Nº: None
Year Formed: 1935
Location: Waltham, near Grimsby
Length of Line: 1,300 feet for 7¼ and 5 inch gauges, 600 feet for 3½ inch gauge

Nº of Steam Locos: 1 (+ members' locos)
Nº of Other Locos: 2
Approx Nº of Visitors P.A.: 10,000
Gauge: 3½ inches, 5 inches & 7¼ inches
Website: www.gcmes.com

GENERAL INFORMATION

Nearest Mainline Station: Grimsby Town (3 miles)
Nearest Bus Station: Grimsby (3 miles)
Car Parking: Available on site
Coach Parking: Limited space available but can be accommodated
Food & Drinks: Available at the Windmill site

SPECIAL INFORMATION

The Society's track is based in Waltham, on the outskirts of Grimsby, next to a preserved windmill dating back to 1878 (the third built on the site since 1666!) which still operates from time to time.

OPERATING INFORMATION

Opening Times: 2024 dates: Sundays and Bank Holidays from 16th March to 3rd November. Trains run from 12.00pm to 4.00pm. A special three-day open gala is held over the August Bank Holiday weekend. The railway also runs on Boxing Day and New Year's Day, offering free train rides from 11.00am to 3.00pm. Please check the web site for further details.
Steam Working: Most operating days.
Prices: From £1.50 per ride

Detailed Directions by Car:
The Railway is situated by Waltham Windmill on the B1203 Grimsby to Binbrook Road and is well signposted. The B1203 connects to the A16 at Scartho, a suburb of Grimsby, about a mile from the railway or to the A18 at Ashby Top, about 3 miles away.

GROSVENOR PARK MINIATURE RAILWAY

Address: Grosvenor Park, Chester, CH1 1QQ
Telephone N°: 07961 099572
Year Formed: 1996
Length of Line: ¼ mile

N° of Steam Locos: None at present
N° of Other Locos: 2
Approx N° of Visitors P.A.: 60,000
Gauge: 7¼ inches
E-mail: gpmrailway@gmail.com

GENERAL INFORMATION

Nearest Mainline Station: Chester (¾ mile)
Nearest Bus Station: Chester (½ mile)
Car Parking: Park & Ride or Public car parks only
Coach Parking: None
Souvenir Shop(s): Yes
Food & Drinks: Available in the Park Cafe

SPECIAL INFORMATION

Grosvenor Park railway was built in 1996 to commemorate the centenary of the Duke of Westminster's railway at nearby Eaton Hall and is located just a few minutes walk from Chester's historic city centre.

OPERATING INFORMATION

Opening Times: 2024 dates: Wednesdays and Fridays from 1st April to 30th September from 10.00am to 5.00 pm (until 4.00pm in the Winter).
Steam Working: None at present.
Prices: Adults £1.50
Children £1.00
Family £3.50

Detailed Directions by Car:
From All Parts: Grosvenor Park is situated in the centre of Chester, by Grosvenor Park Road and about 400 yards from the City Centre. The Roman Amphitheatre is adjacent to the Park.

HALTON MINIATURE RAILWAY

Address: Palace Fields, Town Park, Runcorn WA7 6PT	**N⁰ of Steam Locos:** Members locos only
Telephone N⁰: (01928) 701965	**N⁰ of Other Locos:** 4
Year Formed: 1979	**Approx N⁰ of Visitors P.A.:** 12,500
Location of Line: Runcorn	**Gauge:** 7¼ inches
Length of Line: 1 mile approximately	**Website:** www.haltonminirail.weebly.com

GENERAL INFORMATION

Nearest Mainline Station: Runcorn East (¾ mile)
Nearest Bus Station: Runcorn (¾ mile)
Car Parking: Available on site
Coach Parking: Available
Souvenir Shop(s): None
Food & Drinks: Available at the adjacent Ski Centre

SPECIAL INFORMATION

The railway is operated by the Halton Miniature Railway Society and one of their locomotives, the Norton Priory (illustrated above), was built by schoolchildren from Norton Priory Secondary School in 1983! It has recently been restored to its former glory and is again in regular service.

OPERATING INFORMATION

Opening Times: Sundays and Bank Holidays from April to September plus some other days in August. Trains run from 1.00pm to 4.00pm.
Steam Working: Occasional dates only. Please contact the railway for further details.
Prices: There is no charge to ride the train but donations to help cover costs are welcome.

Detailed Directions by Car:
From All Parts: Exit the M56 at Junction 11 and follow the brown tourist signs for the Ski Centre which is adjacent to the railway.

HARLINGTON LOCOMOTIVE SOCIETY

Address: High Street, Harlington, Hayes, Middlesex UB3 5DF	**N° of Steam Locos:** 40 (Members' locos)
Telephone N°: None	**N° of Other Locos:** Several
Year Formed: 1947	**Approx N° of Visitors P.A.:** 3,000
Location of Line: Harlington High Street	**Gauge:** 3½ inches and 5 inches
Length of Line: 1,047 feet	**Website:**
	www.harlingtonlocomotivesociety.org.uk

GENERAL INFORMATION

Nearest Mainline Station: Hayes (1½ miles)
Nearest Bus Stop: 50 yards – Services 90, H98 & 140
Car Parking: Limited on site parking. Street parking is also available.
Coach Parking: None
Food & Drinks: Light refreshments are available

SPECIAL INFORMATION

Approximately 40 Steam plus several Electric locos are owned by individual members. Typically 4 locos will be in steam on most open days.

OPERATING INFORMATION

Opening Times: 2024 dates: 31st March; 14th April; 12th May; 9th June; 14th July; 11th August; 8th September; 13th October and 8th December (Mince Pie Runs).
Steam Working: Every operating day.
Prices: £1.00 per ride (Under-3s accompanied by a paying adult ride free of charge).

Detailed Directions by Car:
Exit the M25 at Junction 14, initially following signs for Heathrow. At the first roundabout, turn left onto the A3044 towards the A4, passing the new Terminal 5 building on the right hand side. On reaching the A4 turn right towards London. After 2½ miles, at Harlington Corner, turn left onto the A437. The Railway is situated in Harlington village centre on the right, approximately 75 yards after crossing over the mini-roundabout.

HEATH PARK MINIATURE RAILWAY

Address: King George V Drive East, Heath Park, Cardiff   CF14 4AW
Telephone N°: (029) 2025-5000
Year Formed: 1948
Location of Line: Heath Park, Cardiff
Length of Line: 2 tracks of 1,000 feet each plus a tram track of 700 feet

N° of Steam Locos: 8   (plus many
N° of Other Locos: 4   members locos)
Approx N° of Visitors P.A.: 12,000
Gauge: 3½ inches, 5 inches & 7¼ inches
Website: www.cardiffmes.co.uk
E-mail: secretary@cardiffmes.co.uk

GENERAL INFORMATION

Nearest Mainline Station: Heath Low Level (½ mile)
Nearest Bus Stop: Allensbank Road
Car Parking: Available on site and also nearby
Coach Parking: None
Food & Drinks: Available

SPECIAL INFORMATION

The Cardiff Model Engineering society moved to Heath Park in 1987. The site, which includes two railway tracks and a unique electric tramway, an '00' gauge model railway, a garden railway catering for 32mm & 45mm gauges and extensive refreshment facilities, has been developed by the members for the benefit of visitors.

OPERATING INFORMATION

Opening Times: 2024 public running days:
10th & 31st March; 1st & 28th April; 26th & 27th May; 30th June; 21st July; 25th & 26th August; 22nd September; 13th October.
Trains run from 1.00pm to 5.00pm.
Steam Working: All operating days.
Prices: £2.80 entry per person then £2.80 per ride. Children aged 3 and under are admitted and ride free of charge.
Note: Card payments only.

Detailed Directions by Car:
Exit the M4 at Junction 32 and travel towards Cardiff. Turn left at the 3rd set of traffic lights (by the Tesco garage) and continue through 3 sets of traffic lights to the T-junction lights. Turn left here then immediately right then take the 1st left onto King George V Drive. Turn left at the roundabout and take the lane 400 yards on the right.

HILCOTE VALLEY MINIATURE RAILWAY

Address: Fletchers Garden Centre, Bridge Farm, Stone Road, Eccleshall, ST21 6JY
Telephone Nº: (01785) 851057
Year Formed: 1993
Location of Line: Eccleshall, Staffordshire
Length of Line: 500 yards

Nº of Steam Locos: 2
Nº of Other Locos: 2
Approx Nº of Visitors P.A.: 5,000+
Gauge: 7¼ inches
Website: www.hilcotevalleyrailway.co.uk

GENERAL INFORMATION

Nearest Mainline Station: Stafford (6 miles)
Nearest Bus Station: Stafford (6 miles)
Car Parking: Available on site
Coach Parking: Available
Souvenir Shop(s): None
Food & Drinks: Available on site

SPECIAL INFORMATION

Railway enthusiast Roger Greatrex designed and built this railway himself!

OPERATING INFORMATION

Opening Times: Weekends and Bank Holidays from February half term until the end of October and also open during the School Holidays. Trains run from 11.00am to 4.00pm.
Steam Working: Occasional Sundays only, weather permitting.
Prices: £2.00 per ride

Detailed Directions by Car:
From All Parts: Exit the M6 at Junction 14 and take the A5013 to Eccleshall. Just after the junction with the A519, turn right onto the B5026 Stone Road and the Garden Centre is on the right at Bridge Farm after ¾ mile.

HOLLYCOMBE – STEAM IN THE COUNTRY

Address: Iron Hill, Midhurst Road, Liphook, Hants. GU30 7LP
Telephone Nº: (01428) 724900
Year Formed: 1971
Location of Line: Hollycombe, Liphook
Length of Line: 1½ miles of 2 feet gauge and a third of a mile of 7¼ inch gauge

Nº of Steam Locos: 6
Nº of Other Locos: 2
Approx Nº of Visitors P.A.: 25,000
Gauge: 2 feet and 7¼ inches
Website: www.hollycombe.co.uk
E-mail: info@hollycombe.co.uk

GENERAL INFORMATION

Nearest Mainline Station: Liphook (1 mile)
Nearest Bus Station: Liphook
Car Parking: Extensive grass area
Coach Parking: Hardstanding
Souvenir Shop(s): Yes
Food & Drinks: Yes – Cafe

SPECIAL INFORMATION

The narrow gauge railway ascends to spectacular views of the Downs and is part of an extensive working steam museum.

OPERATING INFORMATION

Opening Times: 2024 dates: Sundays and Bank Holidays from 5th May to 20th October. Also open most days in August (until 30th August).
Steam Working: Please contact the museum for further information.
Prices: Adult £25.00
Child £20.00 (under 3s free)
Family £80.00 (2 adults + 2 children)
(Above prices are for unlimited rides on the day)

Detailed Directions by Car:
Take the A3 to Liphook and follow the brown tourist signs for the museum.

ICKENHAM MINIATURE RAILWAY

Correspondence: 25 Copthall Road East, Ickenham, Middlesex UB10 8SD	**N° of Steam Locos**: Up to 6
Telephone N°: (01895) 630125	**N° of Other Locos**: Up to 6
Year Formed: 1948	**Approx N° of Visitors P.A.**: 9,000
Location: At the rear of the "Coach and Horses" Public House, Ickenham	**Gauge**: 3½ inches and 5 inches
Length of Line: 1,100 feet	**Website**: www.idsme.co.uk

GENERAL INFORMATION

Nearest Mainline Station: West Ruislip (½ mile)
Nearest Underground Station: Ickenham (¼ mile)
Car Parking: Public car park is adjacent
Coach Parking: None
Food & Drinks: Available

SPECIAL INFORMATION

The Railway is operated by volunteers from the Ickenham & District Society of Model Engineers.

OPERATING INFORMATION

Opening Times: 2024 dates: The first Saturday of the month from 6th April to 7th December inclusive. Trains run from 12.00pm to 5.30pm (and until dusk later in the year).
Steam Working: All operating days, subject to availability.
Prices: £1.00 per ride.

Detailed Directions by Car:
The Railway is located in Ickenham Village behind the Coach and Horses Public House which is adjacent to the junction of the B466 Ickenham High Road, B466 Long Lane and the B467 Swakeleys Road. From the East: Exit the A40 at Hillingdon Circus turning right onto the B466 Long Lane towards Ickenham/Ruislip. Continue for 1 mile and turn right into Community Close for the car park just before the Coach and Horses in the centre of Ickenham; From the West: Exit the A40 at Hillingdon Circus turning left onto B466 Long Lane. Then as above.

ILFORD & WEST ESSEX MODEL RAILWAY CLUB

Address: Station Road, Chadwell Heath, Romford, Essex RM6 4BU	**Nº of Steam Locos:** 2
Telephone Nº: (01708) 701290	**Nº of Other Locos:** 3
Year Formed: 1930	**Approx Nº of Visitors P.A.:** 500
Location of Line: Chadwell Heath	**Gauge:** 7¼ inches
Length of Line: 150 yards	**Website:** www.iwemrc.org.uk

GENERAL INFORMATION

Nearest Mainline Station: Chadwell Heath (adjacent)
Nearest Bus Station: Chadwell Heath (100 yards)
Car Parking: None on site but a public car park is 100 yards away
Coach Parking: None
Food & Drinks: Light refreshments are available

SPECIAL INFORMATION

The Ilford & West Essex Model Railway Club was formed in 1930 and as such is one of the oldest clubs of its type in the country. Please note that access to the site is by steps only and it is therefore not suitable for wheelchairs.

OPERATING INFORMATION

Opening Times: 2024 dates: The first Sunday of the month from 6th April to 6th October inclusive. Please contact the railway for further information. Trains run from 10.30am to 4.00pm.
Steam Working: When available.
Prices: £1.00 per ride or £4.00 for an all-day pass

Detailed Directions by Car:
The site is alongside Chadwell Heath mainline station just off the A118 between Romford and Ilford town centres. Station Road is to the South of the A118 approximately half-way between the two towns. The site itself is approximately 200 yards down Station Road with a car park on the right hand side.

KEIGHLEY & DISTRICT M.E.S.

Year Formed: 1950
Location of Line: Marley Coaching &
Activities Centre, Keighley   BD21 4DB
Length of Line: 1,500 feet
Website: www.kdmes.org.uk
E-mail: trains@kdmes.org.uk

N° of Steam Locos: 12
N° of Other Locos: 7
Approx N° of Visitors P.A.: 500 – 1,000
Gauge: 3½ inches and 5 inches (raised)

GENERAL INFORMATION

Nearest Mainline Station: Keighley (1 mile)
Nearest Bus Station: Keighley (1½ miles)
Car Parking: Available on site
Coach Parking: None
Food & Drinks: Available

SPECIAL INFORMATION

Keighley & District Model Engineering Society
holds regular public open days at their railway which
is situated by the Marley Activities and Coaching
Centre in Keighley. Please contact the Society for
further details.

OPERATING INFORMATION

Opening Times: 2024 dates: Open days are held on
the third Sunday of the month from 21st April to
28th October. Trains run from 1.30pm to 5.00pm
on open days.
Mince Pie Specials also run on 28th December.
Steam Working: Most operating days.
Prices: £1.00 per person for two circuits of the
track.

Detailed Directions by Car:
From Bradford: Take the A650 towards Keighley. Upon reaching Keighley (with the Marley Leisure Centre on the
right) take the 4th exit at the roundabout into the car park then follow the signs for the railway; From Skipton:
Take the A629 and follow signs for Bradford onto Aire Valley Road. Pass the Beeches Hotel on the right and take
the 2nd exit at the next roundabout into the Activities Centre Car Park for the railway.

KINVER MINIATURE RAILWAY

Year Formed: 1961	**N° of Steam Locos:** 1 + Members locos
Location of Line: Marsh Playing Fields,	**N° of Other Locos:** 2 + Members locos
Kinver, Staffordshire	**Gauge:** 3½ inches , 5 inches & 7¼ inches
Length of Line: ½ mile	**Website:** www.kinvermodelengineers.org.uk
	E-mail: kinver-railway@outlook.com

GENERAL INFORMATION

Nearest Mainline Station: Kidderminster (6 miles)
Nearest Bus Station: Stourbridge (3 miles)
Car Parking: Available on site
Coach Parking: Available on site
Food & Drinks: None

SPECIAL INFORMATION

The railway is operated by the Kinver & West Midlands Society of Model Engineers dates back to organisations formed in the 1920s and has operated a railway in Kinver since 1962.

OPERATING INFORMATION

Opening Times: Most Sunday afternoons between 6th April and 3rd November, weather permitting. Trains run between 2.00pm and approximately 4.30pm. Please check the web site for further information.
Steam Working: Most operating days.
Prices: £2.00 per ride. (under 2s free)

Detailed Directions by Car:
The Society's tracksite is situated on the Marsh Playing Fields at the end of the High Street in the village of Kinver which is to the West of Stourbridge and to the North of Kidderminster.

LAKESHORE RAILROAD

Address: South Marine Park, South Shields NE33 2NN	**N^o of Steam Locos:** 2

Address: South Marine Park,
South Shields NE33 2NN
Correspondence: 6 Marina Drive,
South Shields NE33 2NH
Telephone N^o: 07745 350983
Year Formed: 1972
Length of Line: 570 yards

N^o of Steam Locos: 2
N^o of Other Locos: 1
Approx N^o of Visitors P.A.: 65,000
Gauge: 9½ inches
Website: www.lakeshorerailroad.co.uk
E-mail: info@lakeshorerailroad.co.uk

GENERAL INFORMATION

Nearest Mainline Station: South Shields (¾ mile)
Nearest Bus Station: South Shields (1 mile)
Car Parking: Available on the seafront
Coach Parking: Available nearby
Souvenir Shop(s): None
Food & Drinks: Available nearby

SPECIAL INFORMATION

The Lakeshore Railroad runs two American-designed locomotives – hence the name!

OPERATING INFORMATION

Opening Times: Weekends throughout the year and daily from mid-May to mid-September and during other School Holidays except for Christmas.
Trains run from 11.00am to 5.00pm (until 6.00pm during the summer months).
Steam Working: Daily, subject to availability
Prices: Adults £2.00
Children £2.00 (Free for Under-3s)

Detailed Directions by Car:
From All Parts: Take the A194 into South Shields. The railway is located by the Seafront in South Marine Park and can be found by following the brown tourist signs marked for the 'Seafront'.

LANGFORD & BEELEIGH RAILWAY

Address: Museum of Power,
Hatfield Road, Langford, Maldon, Essex,
CM9 6QA
Telephone Nº: (01621) 843183
Year Formed: 2003
Length of Line: ¼ mile loop

Nº of Steam Locos: 4
Nº of Other Locos: 1
Approx Nº of Visitors P.A.: 6,000
Gauge: 7¼ inches
Website: www.museumofpower.org.uk

GENERAL INFORMATION

Nearest Mainline Station: Witham (4 miles)
Nearest Bus Station: Chelmsford (6 miles)
Car Parking: Available on site
Coach Parking: Available
Souvenir Shop(s): Yes
Food & Drinks: Available

SPECIAL INFORMATION

The Railway is situated at the Museum of Power
which is housed in the Steam Pumping Station at
Langford in Essex. The Museum was set up to
exhibit and demonstrate working examples of power
sources of all types and chronicle the major roles
that they have played in history.

OPERATING INFORMATION

Opening Times: 2024 dates: 31st March;
7th and 28th April; 5th May; 4th August;
1st and 22nd September; 13th October;
30th November and 1st December.
Please contact the Museum for further information.
Steam Working: On all operating days.
Note: On most operating days, visitors must pay for
admission to the Museum to access train tides:
  £10.00 (Adult)
  £9.00 (Concessions)
  £5.00 (Children)
Prices: Adults £2.00 per ride
  Children £1.00 per ride
  Family Ticket £5.00 per ride

Detailed Directions by Car:
The Museum is situated in Langford, on the B1019 Maldon to Hatfield Peverel Road. From the A12, take the
Hatfield Peverel exit, pass through the village and take the B1019 Hatfield Road towards Ulting & Maldon. The
Museum is on the right hand side after approximately 3 miles on the outskirts of Langford.

LITTLEDOWN MINIATURE RAILWAY

Address: Littledown Park, Chaseside, Castle Lane East, Bournemouth, BH7 7DX
Contact Telephone Nº: 07879 355399
Year Formed: 1924
Location of Line: Littledown Park
Length of Line: Over one third of a mile

Nº of Steam Locos: 15+
Nº of Other Locos: 10+
Approx Nº of Visitors P.A.: 4,000
Gauge: 3½ inches, 5 inches & 7¼ inches
Website: www.littledownrailway.org.uk

GENERAL INFORMATION

Nearest Mainline Station:
Bournemouth Central (3½ miles)
Nearest Bus Station: Bournemouth
Car Parking:
In Littledown Leisure Centre car park
Coach Parking: As above

SPECIAL INFORMATION

Bournemouth and District Society of Model Engineers operate the railway at Littledown Park. The society also operates a 16mm garden railway alongside the track.

OPERATING INFO

Opening Times: Most Sundays, Bank Holidays and Wednesdays throughout the year subject to weather conditions. Trains run from 11.00am to 3.00pm.
Steam Working: Subject to availability. Please contact the railway for further information.
Prices: £1.00 per ride.
£10.00 for 15 rides

Detailed Directions by Car:
The Railway is situated at Littledown Park which is to the North-East of Bournemouth town centre close (and to the South of) the junction of Wessex Way (A338) and Castle Lane (A3060).

LITTLE WESTERN RAILWAY

Address: Trenance Gardens, Trenance Road, Newquay TR7 2HL
Year Formed: 1965
Location of Line: Newquay, Cornwall
Length of Line: 480 yards

Nº of Steam Locos: 1
Nº of Other Locos: 4
Approx Nº of Visitors P.A.: Not known
Gauge: 7¼ inches
Website: www.littlewesternrailway.com
E-mail: info@littlewesternrailway.com

GENERAL INFORMATION

Nearest Mainline Station: Newquay (½ mile)
Nearest Bus Station: Newquay (½ mile)
Car Parking: Available on site
Coach Parking: Available
Souvenir Shop(s): Yes
Food & Drinks: Available

SPECIAL INFORMATION

The railway runs through the floral oasis of Trenance Gardens close to Newquay Zoo and is the oldest 7½ inch railway in Cornwall.

OPERATING INFORMATION

Opening Times: 2024 dates: Weekends and school holidays from 29th March to 19th May then daily from 20th May to 15th September. Then weekends and school holidays again until 3rd November. Also 27th December to 1st January.
Steam Working: None at present.
Prices: Adults £1.50 (2 laps of the track)
£12.00 for 10 ride tickets

Detailed Directions by Car:
From All Parts: Take the A30 then the A392 to Newquay. At the roundabout turn right to continue along Trevemper Road which becomes the A3058. Turn left into Trenance Road and the gardens are a little way along.

MIZENS MINIATURE RAILWAY

Address: Barrs Lane, Knaphill, Woking, Surrey GU21 2JW
Telephone N°: (020) 8890-1978
Year Formed: 1989
Location of Line: Knaphill, Surrey
Length of Line: 1 mile
Website: www.wokingminiaturerailwaysociety.com

N° of Steam Locos: 10
N° of Other Locos: 16
Approx N° of Visitors P.A.: 20,000
Gauge: 7¼ inches
E-mail: mizensrailway@rjjagriff.me

GENERAL INFORMATION

Nearest Mainline Station: Woking (2½ miles)
Nearest Bus Station: Woking
Car Parking: 175 spaces available on site
Coach Parking: Available on site but advance notification of the visit is necessary.
Souvenir Shop(s): Yes
Food & Drinks: Tea shop open on running days

SPECIAL INFORMATION

Operated by the Woking Miniature Railway Society, Mizens is situated in a beautiful location amidst 9 acres of woodland and takes its name from Mizens Farm which was its original location but is now the headquarters of the McLaren F1 team!

OPERATING INFORMATION

Opening Times: 2024 dates: Easter Sunday then every Sunday from 5th May to 29th September (except 21st July).
Santa Specials run on 1st, 8th & 15th December. Please check the web site for further details.
Trains operate from 2.00pm to 5.00pm.
Steam Working: Most operating days
Prices: Adult Return From £2.50 or £3.00
Child Return From £2.50 or £3.00
Note: Prices vary depending on the route and Santa Specials must be pre-booked.

Detailed Directions by Car:
From All Parts: Exit the M25 at Junction 11 and follow the A320 to Woking. At the Six Cross Roads Roundabout take the 5th exit towards Knaphill then turn left at the roundabout onto Littlewick Road. Continue along Littlewick Road crossing the roundabout before turning right into Barrs Lane just before Knaphill.

MOORS VALLEY RAILWAY

Address: Moors Valley Country Park, Horton Road, Ashley Heath, Nr. Ringwood, Hants. BH24 2ET **Telephone Nº:** (01425) 471415 **Year Formed:** 1985 **Location:** Moors Valley Country Park	**Length of Line:** 1 mile **Nº of Steam Locos:** 19 **Nº of Other Locos:** 2 **Approx Nº of Visitors P.A.:** 100,000 **Gauge:** 7¼ inches **Website:** www.moorsvalleyrailway.co.uk

GENERAL INFORMATION

Nearest Mainline Station: Bournemouth (12 miles)
Nearest Bus Station: Ringwood (3 miles)
Car Parking: Parking charges vary throughout the year. Maximum charge £12.00 per day.
Coach Parking: Charges are applied for parking
Souvenir Shop(s): Yes + Model Railway Shop
Food & Drinks: Yes

SPECIAL INFORMATION

The Moors Valley Railway is a complete small Railway with signalling and 2 signal boxes in addition to 4 tunnels and 2 level crossings.

OPERATING INFORMATION

Opening Times: 2024 dates: Weekends and school holidays throughout the year. Daily from 25th May to 8th September and during the school holidays. Also Santa Specials in December and occasional other openings. Please phone the Railway or check the website for details.
Steam Working: 10.45am to 5.00pm when open.
Prices: Adult Return £5.15
Child Return £3.55 (under 2s free)
Adult Day Rover £14.95
Child Day Rover £11.95
Special rates are available for parties of 10 or more.

Detailed Directions by Car:
From All Parts: Moors Valley Country Park is situated on Horton Road which is off the A31 Ferndown to Ringwood road near the junction with the A338 to Bournemouth.

NESS ISLANDS RAILWAY

Address: Whin Park, Inverness IV3 5SS	**N⁰ of Steam Locos:** 1
Telephone N⁰: (01463) 235533	**N⁰ of Other Locos:** 2
Year Formed: 1983	**Approx N⁰ of Visitors P.A.:** 12,000
Location of Line: Inverness	**Gauge:** 7¼ inches
Length of Line: 900 yards	**Website:** www.nessislandsrailway.co.uk

GENERAL INFORMATION

Nearest Mainline Station: Inverness (2 miles)
Nearest Bus Station: Inverness (2 miles)
Car Parking: Available on site
Coach Parking: Available
Souvenir Shop(s): Yes
Food & Drinks: None

SPECIAL INFORMATION

Ness Islands Railway is Britain's most northerly 7¼ inch gauge line and is now owned and operated by the Highland Hospice.

OPERATING INFORMATION

Opening Times: 2024 dates: Weekends 31st March to the end of October and also daily during the school holidays.
Trains run from 11.30am to 4.30pm.
Steam Working: Most weekends.
Prices: £3.00 per ride   (Under-4s ride for free)

Detailed Directions by Car:
From All Parts: The Railway is located in Inverness, just to the south of the A82 Glenurquhart Road. Turn into Bught Road at Queens Park and the railway is on the right after a short distance.

NORTH SCARLE MINIATURE RAILWAY

Address: North Scarle Playing Field, Swinderby Road, North Scarle, Lincolnshire LN6 9ER (for SatNav)
Telephone Nº: (01427) 881698
Location of Line: North Scarle, between Newark and Lincoln
Length of Line: A third of a mile

Year Formed: 1933
Nº of Steam Locos: 7
Nº of Other Locos: 8
Approx Nº of Visitors P.A.: 3,000
Gauges: 7¼ inches and 5 inches
Website: www.lincolnmes.co.uk

GENERAL INFORMATION

Nearest Mainline Station: Newark Northgate (5 miles)
Nearest Bus Station: Newark (5 miles)
Car Parking: 300 spaces available on site
Coach Parking: None available
Souvenir Shop(s): None
Food & Drinks: Available on special days only

SPECIAL INFORMATION

The Railway is owned and operated by the Lincoln and District Model Engineering Society which was founded in 1933.

OPERATING INFORMATION

Opening Times: Dates for 2024: The following Sundays: 7th & 21st April; 5th & 19th May; 16th & 30th June; 14th & 28th July; 11th & 25th August; 8th & 22nd September, when trains run from 9.00am to 12.00pm. Also the following Saturdays: 6th & 20th July; 3rd, 17th & 31st August from 2.00pm to 4.00pm. An open weekend is to be held on 28th & 29th September.
Steam Working: Every running day.
Prices: Adult Return £1.50
Child Return £1.50

Detailed Directions by Car:
North Scarle is situated off the A46 between Lincoln and Newark (about 5 miles from Newark). Alternatively, take the A1133 from Gainsborough and follow the North Scarle signs when around 6 miles from Newark.

Northampton Society of Model Engineers

Telephone No: 07763 149241	**No of Steam Locos:** Up to 9 running
Year Formed: 1933	**No of Other Locos:** 4 to 6 run occasionally
Location of Line: Lower Delapre Park,	**Approx No of Visitors P.A.:** 10,000
London Road, Northampton NN4 8AJ	**Gauge:** 3½ inches, 5 inches & 7¼ inches
Length of Line: 1,740 feet (raised track)	**Website:** www.nsme.co.uk
and 3,034 feet (ground level track)	**E-mail:** secretary@nsme.co.uk

GENERAL INFORMATION

Nearest Mainline Station: Northampton (2 miles)
Nearest Bus Station: Northampton (2 miles)
Car Parking: Available on site
Coach Parking: On London Road
Food & Drinks: Light refreshments are available

SPECIAL INFORMATION

The Northampton Society of Model Engineers is a long established society with excellent facilities for model engineers. The society has over 140 members with wide ranging interests, several of whom have won major awards at National exhibitions.

The two tracks were extended during 2011 and are located in a woodland setting with a new garden railway and a picnic site. The site may be hired for Birthday parties on Tuesdays and Saturdays. Please check the web site for further information.

OPERATING INFORMATION

Opening Times: 2024 Dates: 6th May; 2nd June; 7th July; 4th August; 1st September; 6th October. Trains run from 2.00pm to 5.00pm.
Steam Working: Every operating day.
Prices: £1.50 per ride

Detailed Directions by Car:
From the M1: Exit at Junction 15 and take the A508 to Northampton. Take the 2nd turn off onto the A45 (for the Town Centre) and then the 2nd exit at the roundabout. After ½ mile turn right just before the pelican crossing and immediately turn left through the steel gate onto the access track for the railway; From the East: Follow the A45 and take the turn off signposted for Daventry and the Town Centre. Take the 4th exit at the roundabout onto the A508, then as above; From the Town Centre: Take the A508 South (Bridge Street). Cross the river and go straight on at the traffic lights. Pass a petrol station on the left and immediately after the pelican crossing turn left then immediately left again for the railway.

PINEWOOD MINIATURE RAILWAY

Address: Pinewood Leisure Centre, Old Wokingham Road, Wokingham, Berkshire RG40 3AQ **Year Formed:** 1984 **Location:** Pinewood Leisure Centre **Length of Line:** 800 metres	**Nº of Steam Locos:** 17 (All owned **Nº of Other Locos:** 10 by Members) **Approx Nº of Visitors P.A.:** 3,000 **Gauge:** 5 inches and 7¼ inches **Website:** www.pinewoodrailway.co.uk **E-mail:** secretary@pinewoodrailway.co.uk

GENERAL INFORMATION

Nearest Mainline Station: Bracknell
Nearest Bus Station: Bracknell
Car Parking: Available on site
Coach Parking: Available by arrangement
Souvenir Shop(s): None
Food & Drinks: Light refreshments are available

SPECIAL INFORMATION

The Pinewood Miniature Railway runs through attractive woodlands backing on to a Leisure Centre.

OPERATING INFORMATION

Opening Times: 2024 dates: Public running on the 3rd Sunday in the month from March to October. Santa Specials on two Sundays in December (pre-booking is required for these dates). Private Parties can sometimes be catered for by prior arrangement. Trains run from 1.30pm to 4.00pm.
Steam Working: All open days.
Prices: £1.50 per ride or 4 rides for £5.00
Note: Under-3s ride free of charge

Detailed Directions by Car:
From the M3 or the A30 take the A322 towards Bracknell. Once on the A322, keep in the left hand lane to the first major roundabout then take the first exit onto the B3430 towards Wokingham along Nine Mile Ride. Cross the next roundabout (A3095) and continue on the B3430 passing the Golden Retriever pub and the Crematorium. Go straight on at the next mini-roundabout then turn right at the following roundabout into Old Wokingham Road. The Pinewood Leisure Centre is on the left after approximately 100 metres.

PLYMOUTH MINIATURE STEAM

Address: Goodwin Park, Pendeen Crescent, Southway, Plymouth PL6 6RE	**N⁰ of Steam Locos:** 2 + member locos
Phone N⁰: (01752) 661780 (Secretary)	**N⁰ of Other Locos:** 2 + member locos
Year Formed: 1990	**Approx N⁰ of Visitors P.A.:** 2,000
Location of Line: Goodwin Park Public Nature Reserve	**Gauge:** 3½ inches, 5 inches & 7¼ inches
Length of Line: ½ mile	**Website:** www.plymouthminiaturesteam.co.uk

GENERAL INFORMATION

Nearest Mainline Station: Plymouth (6 miles)
Nearest Bus Station: Plymouth (6 miles)
Car Parking: Available on site (limited headroom)
Coach Parking: None
Food & Drinks: Light refreshments available.

SPECIAL INFORMATION

The railway runs through Goodwin Park, a site specially developed by members of the Society which was opened in 1990 and has since been designated as a Public Nature Reserve.

OPERATING INFORMATION

Opening Times: Open during the 1st and 3rd Sunday afternoons of each month from April to October inclusive, from 2.00pm to 4.30pm.
Steam Working: Most operating days.
Prices: £1.00 per ride. (under 3s free)

Detailed Directions by Car:
From the A38 Plymouth Parkway, follow the signs for Tavistock (A386) travelling North until reaching a new road junction near Plymouth Airport and a Park & Ride site. Turn left at this junction into the Southway Estate and follow the road for ½ mile past two mini-roundabouts and a set of traffic lights. At the 3rd mini-roundabout turn left into Pendeen Crescent and about 200 yard on the right is a signpost for the railway. Follow the lane to the parking area but please note that the bridge has just 6 feet headroom so large vehicles must park outside the track!

POPLAR MINIATURE RAILWAY

Address: Poplar Nurseries, Coggleshall Road, Marks Tey, Near Colchester, CO6 1HR **Telephone Nº:** 07780 603001 **Year Formed:** 2013 **Location:** Poplar Garden Centre **Length of Line:** 350 yards	**Nº of Steam Locos:** 1 **Nº of Other Locos:** 2 **Approx Nº of Visitors P.A.:** 49,000 **Gauge:** 7¼ inches **Website:** www.poplarminirail.co.uk **E-mail:** info@poplarrailway.co.uk

GENERAL INFORMATION

Nearest Mainline Station: Marks Tey (1½ miles)
Nearest Bus Station: Colchester (8 miles) – Service 70 from Colchester to Braintree runs past the site.
Car Parking: Available on site
Coach Parking: Available on site
Souvenir Shop(s): Available
Food & Drinks: Restaurant available on site

SPECIAL INFORMATION

The Railway runs through the gardens of Poplar Nurseries and complements the other attractions of the garden centre which include a restaurant, farm shop and play area.

OPERATING INFORMATION

Opening Times: 2024 dates: Weekends and Bank Holidays from Easter to the end of December. Open daily during Summer school holidays and also for special Halloween and Christmas events in October and December respectively. Please contact the railway for details about these Special Events. Trains run from 10.30am to 4.00pm except for most weekdays from April to the end of July when they run from 10.00am to 2.00pm.
Steam Working: Most operating days.
Prices: £2.00 per person for the first ride then £1.00 for each additional ride that day.
Under-4s travel free of charge but must be accompanied by a paying adult.

Detailed Directions by Car:
From the M11, Stansted and the North: Exit the M11 at Junction 8 and follow the A120 to Marks Tey. Poplar Nurseries is situated on the right hand side of the road; From London and the South: Take the A12 for Colchester then turn off onto the A120 at Junction 25. Follow the A120 and Stansted Airport signs for 1 mile from the junction and Poplar Nurseries is located on the left hand side of the road.

PROSPECT PARK MINIATURE RAILWAY

Address: Prospect Park, 82 Bath Road, Reading, Berkshire RG30 2BJ
Year Formed: 1909 (line since 1975)
Location of Line: Prospect Park, Reading
Length of Line: Two lines, one of 1,100 feet and one of 1,350 feet
Approx Nº of Visitors P.A.: 25,000

Nº of Steam Locos: 2 + members locos
Nº of Other Locos: 5 + members locos
Gauge: 2½ inches, 3½ inches, 5 inches and 7¼ inches
Website: www.rsme.uk
Email: secretary@rsme.uk

GENERAL INFORMATION

Nearest Mainline Station: Reading (2 miles)
Nearest Bus Station: Reading Station (2 miles)
Car Parking: Available on site
Coach Parking: Available by prior arrangement
Souvenir Shop(s): None
Food & Drinks: Available

SPECIAL INFORMATION

The Reading SME has been using the current site for more than 40 years and it now boasts a well equipped club house and useful workshop facilities.

To find the railway on facebook, search for 'Prospect Park Railway – Reading Society of Model Engineers'.

OPERATING INFORMATION

Opening Times: The first Sunday of the month from February to November and also some Bank Holidays. Please check the facebook page for further details. Trains usually run from 12.00pm to 3.30pm (though times can vary during the Winter months).
Steam Working: All operating days
Prices: 60p per ride or 10 rides for £5.00

Detailed Directions by Car:
Exit the M4 at Junction 12 and take the A4 Bath Road towards Reading. Continue on this road for approximately 2¼ miles. Prospect Park is on the left, continue along Bath Road almost to the end of Prospect Park and the entrance to the car park for the railway is on the left about 100 metres before the traffic lights.

PUGNEYS LIGHT RAILWAY

Address: Pugneys Country Park, Denby Dale Road, Wakefield WF2 7EQ	**Nᵒ of Steam Locos:** 2
Telephone Nᵒ: 07885 930523	**Nᵒ of Other Locos:** 6 at present
Year Formed: 1998	**Approx Nᵒ of Visitors P.A.:** 16,000
Location of Line: Pugneys Country Park	**Gauge:** 7¼ inches
Length of Line: 1,400 yards	**Website:** www.pugneyslightrailway.co.uk
	E-mail: contact@pugneyslightrailway.co.uk

GENERAL INFORMATION

Nearest Mainline Station: Wakefield (1½ miles)
Nearest Bus Station: Wakefield (2 miles)
Car Parking: Available on site
Coach Parking: Available by prior arrangement
Souvenir Shop(s): Yes
Food & Drinks: Available

SPECIAL INFORMATION

The railway is steadily improving and developing and is operated by a dedicated group of volunteers. The line runs part way around one of two lakes in Pugneys Country Park, once an open cast mine and gravel quarry, and the journey offers extensive views of Sandal Castle across the main lake. Bike hire, a café, footpaths/cycle paths around the main lake and a children's play area can also be found in the Park.

OPERATING INFORMATION

Opening Times: Weekends and Bank Holidays throughout the year and also during the School Holidays. Open other days by special arrangement. Opening days are weather-dependent so please phone or check the Facebook page before visiting. Open 11.00am to 4.00pm (until 5.00pm during British Summer Time) and often later during Special Events.
Steam Working: Most Sundays plus some Saturdays during the summer months.
Visiting locos occasionally operate on the line.
Prices: £2.00 per journey
Note: Visiting locos are welcome by prior arrangement and Special events can be booked by prior arrangement.

Detailed Directions by Car:
From All Parts: Exit the M1 at Junction 39 and take the A636 towards Wakefield. After approximately 1 mile, turn right at the 2nd roundabout into the Park.

RAINSBROOK VALLEY RAILWAY

Address: Rugby Model Engineering Society, Onley Lane, Rugby CV22 5QD
Telephone Nº: None
Year Formed: 1949
Location of Line: Onley Lane, Rugby
Length of Line: 1,770 yards ground level (7¼ inch) and also 1,100 feet elevated (2½, 3½ & 5 inch gauges)

Nº of Steam Locos: 10
Nº of Other Locos: 4+
Approx Nº of Visitors P.A.: 6,000
Gauges: 2½ inches, 3½ inches, 5 inches & 7¼ inches
Website: www.rugbymes.co.uk
E-mail: secretary@rugbymes.co.uk

GENERAL INFORMATION

Nearest Mainline Station: Rugby (2½ miles)
Nearest Bus Station: Rugby (2½ miles)
Car Parking: Available on site
Coach Parking: None
Souvenir Shop(s): None
Food & Drinks: Light refreshments only

SPECIAL INFORMATION

The Rainsbrook Valley Railway is operated by members of the Rugby Model Engineering Society Ltd.

OPERATING INFORMATION

Opening Times: 2024 dates: Every 3rd Sunday in the month from April to October plus Christmas Trains in December. Trains run over 2 sessions from 11.00am to 1.00pm and from 2.00pm to 4.00pm.
Steam Working: All operating days
Prices: £8.00 for each session

Detailed Directions by Car:
From the M1: Exit at Junction 18 and follow the A428 westwards towards Rugby. After 3 miles turn left on to the B4429 towards Dunchurch. After 1 mile turn left at the crossroads into Onley Lane and the Railway is on the right hand side after 300 yards; From Dunchurch: Follow the A426 Northwards then turn onto the B4429 at the roundabout travelling Eastwards. After 1 mile turn right at the crossroads into Onley Lane for the Railway; From Rugby: In Rugby, follow signs for the Hospital in Barby Road then continue South for 1 mile. At the crossroads go straight on over the B4429 into Onley Lane for the Railway.

RAVENSPRINGS PARK RAILWAY

Address: Ravensprings Park, Cawcliffe Road, Brighouse   HD6 2HP
Telephone Nº: (01484) 717140
Year Formed: 1932
Location of Line: Ravensprings Park
Length of Line: 650 feet (5 inch gauge) and 1,200 feet (7¼ inch gauge)

Nº of Steam Locos: 50-60
Nº of Other Locos: 2 (traction engines)
Approx Nº of Visitors P.A.: 4,500
Gauge: 2½ inches, 3½ inches, 5 inches and 7¼ inches
Website: www.bhme.co.uk

GENERAL INFORMATION

Nearest Mainline Station: Brighouse (1½ miles)
Nearest Bus Station: Brighouse (1 mile)
Car Parking: Available on site
Coach Parking: Available by prior arrangement
Food & Drinks: Available on open days

SPECIAL INFORMATION

The railway is operated by the Brighouse & Halifax Model Engineers Society.

OPERATING INFORMATION

Opening Times: 2024 dates: 14th April; 12th May; 9th June; 14th July; 11th August; 8th September; 13th October.
Trains run from 1.30pm to 5.00pm.
Steam Working: All operating days.
Prices: All tickets must be pre-booked and cost £4.50 each for a 2-hour session.

Detailed Directions by Car:
Ravensprings Park lies in the Northern part of Brighouse. From the South: Take the A641 Bradford Road northwards and turn left just after the Thaal Indian Restaurant into Cross Street for Smith Carr Lane. Turn right into Bracken Road then left into Cawcliffe Road for the Park; From the North: Travel into Brighouse on the A641 and turn right just before the Thaal Indian Restaurant into Cross Street. Then as above.

ROXBOURNE PARK MINIATURE RAILWAY

Address: Roxbourne Park, Field End Road, Eastcote, Ruislip   HA4 9PB
Telephone Nº: None
Year Formed: 1936
Location of Line: Roxbourne Park
Length of Line: 2,200 feet

Nº of Steam Locos: Members locos only
Nº of Other Locos: Members locos only
Approx Nº of Visitors P.A.: 2,500
Gauge: 3½ inches, 5 inches & 7¼ inches
Website: www.hwsme.org
E-mail: info@hwsme.org

GENERAL INFORMATION

Nearest Tube Station: Eastcote (½ mile)
Nearest Bus Station: –
Car Parking: Free parking is available on site
Coach Parking: None
Food & Drinks: None

SPECIAL INFORMATION

The railway is operated by members of the Harrow & Wembley Society of Model Engineers which has been running passenger services on the current track in Roxbourne Park since 1979.

OPERATING INFORMATION

Opening Times: 2024 dates: Every Sunday from 31st March to 20th October inclusive with trains running from 2.30pm to 5.00pm.
A special Halloween train runs on 27th October from 1.00pm to 4.00pm and Father Christmas trains operate on 8th December during the same hours. For details of further special events, please check the society's website.
Steam Working: Every operating day.
Prices: £2.00 per ride

Detailed Directions by Car:
Exit the M40 at Target roundabout and travel into Northolt Village on the A312. Turn left into Eastcote Lane North after the traffic lights just after Northolt Station and continue along this road. Eastcote Lane becomes Field End Road and Roxbourne Park is a little further on opposite Venue '5' (formerly The Clay Pigeon Public House).

ROYDS PARK MINIATURE RAILWAY

Year Formed: 1950	**No of Steam Locos:** 3 (+ members locos)
Location: Royds Park, Cleckheaton, BD19 5LL	**No of Other Locos:** 2 (+ members locos)
	Approx No of Visitors P.A.: 3,000
Length of Line: One tenth of a mile	**Gauge:** 5 inches and 7¼ inches

GENERAL INFORMATION

Nearest Mainline Station: Dewsbury (5 miles)
Nearest Bus Station: Cleckheaton
Car Parking: Approximately 20 spaces on site
Coach Parking: None
Food & Drinks: Light refreshments available

SPECIAL INFORMATION

Spenborough Model & Experimental Engineers operate their service on two tracks in Royds Park which are built on the trackbed of the old London & North West Railway. The club operates a Cromar white carriage for wheelchair passengers.

OPERATING INFORMATION

Opening Times: 2024 dates: 24th & 31st March; 14th & 28th April; 9th & 23rd June; 14th & 28th July; 11th & 25th August; 8th & 22nd September; 13th & 27th October; 10th November. Also Wednesdays during the summer school holidays. Trains run from 12.00pm to 3.00pm on these dates. Mince Pie Specials run on 8th December from 1.00pm to 4.00pm.
Please check the web site for further information.
Steam Working: Most operating days.
Prices: £1.00 per ride (3 circuits of the track).

Detailed Directions by Car:
Exit the M62 at Junction 26 and turn off at the roundabout onto the A638 Cleckheaton to Dewsbury road. Travel through Cleckheaton for approximately ¾ mile then, just after the start of the dual carriageway, turn left onto New Street and at the top of the street is the entrance to Royds Park.

RYEDALE SOCIETY OF MODEL ENGINEERS

Address: The Club House, Pottergate, Gilling East, North Yorkshire   YO62 4JJ
Telephone Nº: None
Year Formed: 1983
Location of Line: Gilling East
Length of Line: 450 metres

Nº of Steam Locos: 10
Nº of Other Locos: Several
Approx Nº of Visitors P.A.: 3,500
Gauge: 3½ inches, 5 inches and 7¼ inches
Website: www.rsme.org.uk

GENERAL INFORMATION
Nearest Mainline Station: Thirsk (11 miles)
Nearest Bus Station: Helmsley (5 miles)
Car Parking: Available on site
Coach Parking: Available
Souvenir Shop(s): None
Food & Drinks: Available

OPERATING INFORMATION
Opening Times: 2024 dates: 7th & 21st April; 5th & 19th May; 4th & 18th June; 7th & 21st July; 4th & 21st August; 1st & 15th September. Open from 12.30pm to 4.30pm.
Steam Working: Every operating day.
Prices: £1.50 per ride

Detailed Directions by Car:
Gilling East is situated approximately 3 miles south of Helmsley (which is on the A170 Thirsk to Scarborough road). Gilling East is on the B1363 which joins the B1257 at nearby Oswaldkirk. Head West at the crossroads by the Fairfax Arms, signposted for the Golf Club and The Old School is situated on the right after around 200 yards.

STANSTED PARK LIGHT RAILWAY

Address: Stansted House,
Rowlands Castle   PO9 6DX
Telephone Nº: (023) 9241-3324
Year Formed: 2005
Location: Stansted House, Hampshire
Length of Line: ½ mile

Nº of Steam Locos: 4
Nº of Other Locos: 3
Approx Nº of Visitors P.A.: 20,000
Gauge: 7¼ inches
Website: www.sp-lr.co.uk
E-mail: help@sp-lr.co.uk

GENERAL INFORMATION

Nearest Mainline Station: Rowlands Castle
(1¼ miles)
Nearest Bus Station: Hilsea Portsmouth (5 miles)
Car Parking: Available on site
Coach Parking: Available
Souvenir Shop(s): At the Garden Centre
Food & Drinks: Available

SPECIAL INFORMATION

The railway is located within the grounds of
Stansted House which stands in 1,800 acres of
ancient forest on the South Downs. The line passes
through the Bessborough Arboretum.

OPERATING INFORMATION

Opening Times: 2024 dates: Wednesdays,
Saturdays and Bank Holidays from 2nd March to
30th October and daily during the School Holidays.
Trains run from 11.00am to 4.00pm.
Steam Working: Most opening days during the
Summer, weather permitting.
Prices: Adults £3.00
        Children £2.00 (Free for Under-2s)

Detailed Directions by Car:
From All Parts: Exit the A3(M) at Junction 2 and take the B2149 towards Rowlands Castle.

Stoke Park Railway

Address: Burchatts Farm, Stoke Park, Guildford, Surrey GU1 1TU
Telephone Nº: None
Year Formed: 1954
Location of Line: Stoke Park, Guildford
Length of Line: 990 feet ground level track and 1,405 feet raised track

Nº of Steam Locos: 6 + visiting locos
Nº of Other Locos: 2
Approx Nº of Visitors P.A.: 10,000
Gauges: 7¼ inches, 5 inches, 3½ inches and 2½ inches
Website: www.gmes.org.uk
E-mail: pr@gmes.org.uk

GENERAL INFO

Nearest Mainline Station:
Guildford London Road (½ mile)
Nearest Bus Station:
Guildford (2½ miles)
Car Parking: Street parking + some available on site
Coach Parking:
Street parking only
Souvenir Shop(s): None
Food & Drinks: Available

SPECIAL INFO

The Guildford Model Engineering Society has operated a miniature railway at the Burchatts Farm site since 1958 and now also has two Garden railways operating on the site.

OPERATING INFO

Opening Times: 2024 Dates: 17th March; 4th & 21st April; 19th & 30th May; 9th June; 6th, 7th & 21st July; 8th, 18th & 29th August; 15th September and 20th & 31st October – open from 2.00pm to 5.00pm on these dates. Also open for the Stoke Park Railway Gala weekend on 6th & 7th July from 10.00am to 5.00pm and a Christmas Special operates on 8th December, 11.00am to 3.00pm.
Steam Working: Every open day.
Prices: 1 ride for £2.00
3 rides for £5.00

Detailed Directions by Car:
The Railway is located at the Eastern end of Stoke Park in Guildford, not far from the Spectrum Sports Centre and near to the junction of the A25 (Parkway) and the A3100 (London Road). Access to the Burchatts Farm site is via London Road.

STRATHAVEN MINIATURE RAILWAY

Address: George Allan Park, Threestanes Road, Strathaven ML10 6EF
Telephone Nº: (01357) 521995
Year Formed: 1949
Location of Line: George Allan Park
Length of Line: 2,270 feet of 5 inch and 7¼ inch gauge on the ground level track. The raised track of 2½ inch, 3½ inch and 5 inch gauges is 408 feet in length

Nº of Steam Locos: 2 (+ Members locos)
Nº of Other Locos: 3
Approx Nº of Visitors P.A.: 12,000
Gauges: 2½ inches, 3½ inches, 5 inches and 7¼ inches
Web: www.strathavenminiaturerailway.org
E-mail: strathavenminiaturerailway@gmail.com

GENERAL INFORMATION

Nearest Mainline Station: Hamilton (8 miles)
Nearest Bus Station: Hamilton (8 miles)
Car Parking: Available on site
Coach Parking: Available
Souvenir Shop(s): None
Food & Drinks: Available in the Park

SPECIAL INFORMATION

The railway is operated by members of the Strathaven Model Society.

OPERATING INFORMATION

Opening Times: Weekends and Bank Holiday Mondays from Easter until the end of September. Trains run from 1.00pm to 4.30pm.
Steam Working: Most operating days, weather permitting.
Prices: £1.00 per ride

Detailed Directions by Car:
From All Parts: Exit the M74 at Junction 8 and take the A71 through Stonehouse to Strathaven. Turn right onto the A726 and George Allan Park is on the left hand side of the road.

STRAWBERRY LINE MINIATURE RAILWAY

Address: Avon Valley Country Park, Pixash Lane, Keynsham, Bristol BS31 1TP
Telephone Nº: (0117) 986-4929
Year Formed: 1999
Location: Avon Valley Country Park
Length of Line: Two-thirds of a mile

Nº of Steam Locos: 5
Nº of Other Locos: 30
Approx Nº of Visitors P.A.: Not known
Gauge: 7¼ & 5 inches
Website: www.avonvalley.co.uk
E-mail: info@avonvalley.co.uk

GENERAL INFORMATION

Nearest Mainline Station: Keynsham (2 miles)
Nearest Bus Station: Bath (6 miles)
Car Parking: Available on site
Coach Parking: Available
Souvenir Shop(s): Yes
Food & Drinks: Available

SPECIAL INFORMATION

The Strawberry Line operates within the Avon Valley Country Park and now has a 7¼-inch gauge line in addition to the extensive 5-inch line.

OPERATING INFORMATION

Opening Times: 2024 dates: Open during School and Bank Holidays from 10.00am to 5.30pm.
Steam Working: Frequently – please contact the railway for further details.
Prices: £2.00 per ride, but see below.
Note: There is a separate admission charge for entry into the Avon Valley Country Park (which is required to access the railway), with prices starting at £14.95 per person.

Detailed Directions by Car:
From All Parts: Take the A4 from Bath or Bristol to Keynsham and turn into Pixash Lane following the brown tourist signs for the Country Park.

SUMMERFIELDS MINIATURE RAILWAYS

Address: Summerfield Barns, High Road, Haynes, Bedford MK45 3BH
Telephone Nº: 07498 869902 (operating days only)
Year Formed: 1948
Location: Off the A600, North of Haynes
Length of Line: Approximately ¾ mile

Nº of Steam Locos: 2 + members locos
Nº of Other Locos: 3 + members locos
Approx Nº of Visitors P.A.: 10,000
Gauge: 3½ inches, 5 inches & 7¼ inches
Website: www.bedfordmes.co.uk

GENERAL INFORMATION

Nearest Mainline Station: Bedford (5½ miles)
Nearest Bus Station: Bedford
Car Parking: Available on site
Coach Parking: Available on site
Souvenir Shop(s): None
Food & Drinks: Available

SPECIAL INFORMATION

Summerfields Miniature Railways is operated by the Bedford Model Engineering Society.

OPERATING INFORMATION

Opening Times: 2024 dates: 31st March; 1st, 10th & 21st April; 5th, 6th, 26th & 27th May; 9th & 23rd June; 7th, 24th & 31st July; 7th, 14th, 25th & 26th August; 1st & 15th September; 6th, 20th & 30th October. Santa Specials run on 30th November & 1st December when advance booking is required. Trains run from 10.30am to 3.30pm.
Steam Working: On all public running days
Prices: Adult Return £3.00
            Child Return £3.00
Note: Under-5s ride free with a paying adult

Detailed Directions by Car:
From All Parts: The Railway is located by the A600 just to the North of Haynes, 5½ miles South of Bedford and 3½ miles North of Shefford.

SURREY SOCIETY OF MODEL ENGINEERS

Address: Mill Lane, Leatherhead, Surrey, KT22 9AA (No post please as the site does not have a letterbox!)
Telephone Nº: None
Year Formed: 1978
Location of Line: Mill Lane, Leatherhead
Length of Line: 2,000 feet

Nº of Steam Locos: 10
Nº of Other Locos: 8
Approx Nº of Visitors P.A.: 15,000
Gauge: Both ground and raised level tracks are available covering many gauges
Website: www.ssme.co.uk
E-mail: enquiries@ssme.co.uk

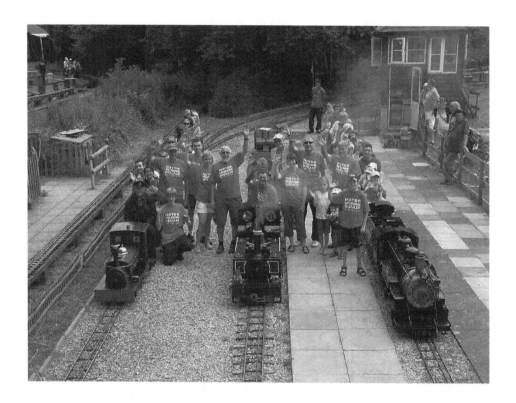

GENERAL INFORMATION

Nearest Mainline Station: Leatherhead (½ mile)
Nearest Bus Station: Leatherhead (½ mile)
Car Parking: Local town centre car parks only – non available on site
Coach Parking: None
Food & Drinks: Available

OPERATING INFORMATION

Opening Times: 2024 dates: 29th March; 14th April; 6th & 27th May; 9th June; 26th August; 8th September; 15th October. Trains run from 11.00am to 4.00pm. Please contact the railway or check their web site for further details.
Steam Working: All operating days.
Prices: £2.00 per ride
£10.00 multi-ride ticket allows 6 rides

Detailed Directions by Car:
The railway is situated near Leatherhead town centre. Mill Lane is across the road from the well signposted Leisure Centre just off the B2122 Waterway Road and just a short walk to the south of Leatherhead Mainline station.

SWANLEY NEW BARN RAILWAY

Address: Swanley Park, New Barn Road, Swanley BR8 7PW	**Nº of Steam Locos:** 7
Telephone Nº: None	**Nº of Other Locos:** 13
Year Formed: 1986	**Approx Nº of Visitors P.A.:** Not known
Location of Line: Swanley, Kent	**Gauge:** 7¼ inches
Length of Line: 900 yards	**Website:** steamdriver.wixsite.com/snbr

GENERAL INFORMATION

Nearest Mainline Station: Swanley (¾ mile)
Nearest Bus Station: Swanley (¾ mile)
Car Parking: Available on site
Coach Parking: Available
Souvenir Shop(s): None
Food & Drinks: Available in the Park

SPECIAL INFORMATION

The railway is located in a Swanley Park which also has play areas, paddling pool, sandpit, boating lake, cafeteria, bouncy castle and battery bikes all set in 60 acres of parkland with free access and parking.

OPERATING INFORMATION

Opening Times: 2024 dates: Weekends and most days during the School Holidays from 29th March to 3rd November.
Trains run from 11.00am to 5.00pm.
Steam Working: Regular steam working but on an ad hoc basis.
Prices: Adult Return £2.00
Child Return £2.00 (Ages 3 to 15)
Note: Lower prices apply for single fares and Under-3s ride for free.

Detailed Directions by Car:
From All Parts: Exit the M25 at Junction 3 and follow green signs for Swanley Park. Go straight on at the first roundabout then turn right at the second roundabout. Continue straight on at the next roundabout then turn left at the next crossroads into New Barn Road. The Park is on the left side of the road.

THAMES DITTON MINIATURE RAILWAY

Address: Willowbank, Claygate Lane, Thames Ditton, Surrey KT7 0LE
Telephone Nº: (020) 8398 3985
Year Formed: 1936
Location of Line: Thames Ditton
Length of Line: ½ mile

Nº of Steam Locos: 30+
Nº of Other Locos: 10+
Approx Nº of Visitors P.A.: 15,000
Gauge: 3½ inches, 5 inches & 7¼ inches
Website: www.malden-dsme.co.uk

GENERAL INFORMATION

Nearest Mainline Station: Thames Ditton (½ mile)
Nearest Bus Station: Thames Ditton
Car Parking: Street parking only
Coach Parking: None
Souvenir Shop(s): Yes
Food & Drinks: Available from 2.30pm onwards

SPECIAL INFORMATION

The railway is operated by Malden and District Society of Model Engineers, is well known locally and is referred to as the Thames Ditton Miniature Railway. The Society operates two tracks at the site – a ground level railway is for larger trains and an elevated railway is for the smaller scale trains. Both are used for passenger hauling services.

OPERATING INFORMATION

Opening Times: Open on Easter Sunday and Monday then the first Sunday of each month and every Bank Holiday Sunday and Monday until the first Sunday in October. Trains run from 2.00pm to 5.30pm though the site is open from 1.00pm onwards. Also open in December for pre-booked Santa Specials – please check the website for further details.
Steam Working: Every operating day.
Prices: Single ride tickets £3.50
Unlimited ride tickets £9.00

Detailed Directions by Car:
Claygate Lane is located just off the A307 Esher to Kingston road about half a mile to the East of the junction between the A307 and A309. If travelling from the East, Claygate Lane is the turning on the left immediately before the railway bridge. If travelling from the West, Claygate Lane is immediately after the second railway bridge though there is unfortunately, no right turn allowed from this direction.

THOMPSON PARK RAILWAY

Location: Thompson Park, Colne Road, Burnley   BB11 2AA
Contact Telephone N°: 07957 714148
Year Formed: 1990
Length of Line: 1 kilometre
Gauge: 7¼ inches

N° of Steam Locos: 3 (Member's locos)
N° of Other Locos: 10
Approx N° of Visitors P.A.: 22,000
Website: www.bpmrs.org.uk
E-mail: Contact via the website

GENERAL INFORMATION

Nearest Mainline Station: Burnley Central (1 mile)
Nearest Bus Station: Burnley (1 mile)
Car Parking: Available
Coach Parking: Not available
Food & Drinks: Available from a kiosk in the Park

SPECIAL INFORMATION

The Railway is operated by the Burnley & Pendle Miniature Railway Society.

OPERATING INFORMATION

Opening Times: 2024 dates: Weekends and Bank Holidays from March until the end of October. Also open on Wednesdays during the School Holidays. Santa Specials run on 7th & 8th December. Trains run between 12.00pm and 4.00pm.
Steam Working: Most operating days.
Prices: Adults £2.00 a ride
Children £1.00 a ride
Families £5.00 (2 adults + 2 children)
Note: 12 rides are available for a flat rate of £10.00.

Detailed Directions by Car:
The Railway runs through Thompson Park in Burnley. The pedestrian entrance is in Ormerod Road, just a short distance from the town centre and also near to Turf Moor, the home of Burnley FC. Cars enter via Colne Road.

THORNES PARK MINIATURE RAILWAY

Address: Thornes Park, Lawefield Lane, Wakefield WF2 8QZ
Telephone Nº: (01924) 457690
Year Formed: 1952
Location: Thornes Park, Wakefield
Length of Line: ½ mile

Nº of Steam Locos: 7
Nº of Other Locos: 4
Approx Nº of Visitors P.A.: 20,000
Gauges: 7¼ inches
Website: www.wakefieldsmee.co.uk

GENERAL INFORMATION

Nearest Mainline Station: Wakefield Westgate (¾ mile)
Nearest Bus Station: Wakefield (1¼ miles)
Car Parking: Available on site
Coach Parking: Available on site
Souvenir Shop(s): None
Food & Drinks: None

SPECIAL INFORMATION

The railway is operated by members of the Wakefield Society of Model and Experimental Engineers. The group is non-profit making and all proceeds after operating costs are donated annually to the Mayor of Wakefield's chosen charity.

OPERATING INFORMATION

Opening Times: Every Sunday (weather permitting) plus Saturdays and Bank Holidays depending on availability of manpower. Trains run from 12.00pm to 4.30pm. Also open for some other special events. Operation is dependent on weather conditions.
Steam Working: Generally whenever the railway is operating.
Prices: Adults £1.00
Children £1.00 (free of charge for infants)

Detailed Directions by Car:
From All Parts: Thornes Park is located approximately 2 miles from Wakefield City Centre, just off the main Huddersfield to Wakefield road (A638).

TONBRIDGE MODEL ENGINEERING SOCIETY

Address: The Slade, Castle Grounds, Tonbridge, Kent   TN9 1HR
Telephone Nº: 07776 161811
Year Formed: 1944
Length of Line: ¼ mile
Nº of Steam Locos: 40

Nº of Other Locos: 10
Approx Nº of Visitors P.A.: 14,000
Gauge: 3½ inches and 5 inches
Website: www.tonbridgemes.com
E-mail: info@tonbridgemes.com

GENERAL INFORMATION

Nearest Mainline Station: Tonbridge (1 mile)
Nearest Bus Station: Tonbridge (1 mile)
Car Parking: Available on site
Coach Parking: None
Food & Drinks: Available at the swimming pool cafe.

SPECIAL INFORMATION

The Society has run a track at the present site since 1951 and since then facilities have been extended to include a steaming bay and turntable, passenger trollies, refreshment facilities and meeting room, store, and a well appointed workshop.

OPERATING INFORMATION

Opening Times: 2024 dates: Saturday and Sunday afternoons from 30th March to 27th October, weather permitting.
Please contact the railway for further information.
Steam Working: Every operating day.
Prices: Free of charge but donations are requested.

Detailed Directions by Car:
Exit the A21 Tonbridge Bypass at the junction signposted for Tonbridge South. Drive up the High Street, cross over the River Medway and turn left by the sign for the Swimming Pool. Follow the road round, turn left at Slade School and the car park for the railway is directly ahead.

URMSTON MINIATURE RAILWAY

Address: Urmston & District MES Ltd, Abbotsfield Park, Chassen Road, Flixton, Manchester M41 5DH
Year Formed: 1948
Location: The Borough of Trafford
Length of Line: 2,200 feet

Nº of Steam Locos: Members' locos only
Nº of Other Locos: Members' locos only
Approx Nº of Visitors P.A.: 5,000+
Gauge: 3½ inches and 5 inches
Website: www.udmes.co.uk

GENERAL INFORMATION

Nearest Mainline Station: Urmston (1 mile) (Chassen Road Station is closer but no trains stop there on Sundays!)
Nearest Bus Station: Central Manchester (7 miles)
Car Parking: Street parking only
Coach Parking: None
Souvenir Shop(s): None
Food & Drinks: Available from an ice cream van

OPERATING INFORMATION

Opening Times: Sundays throughout the year, except for Christmas Day.
Open from approximately 10.30pm to 4.00pm.
Steam Working: Please contact the Society for information.
Prices: 50p per ride

Detailed Directions by Car:
From the North: Exit the M60 at Junction 10 and take the 3rd exit onto the B2514 heading southwards. Continue straight on at two roundabouts passing the Nag's Head pub into Crofts Bank Road. Shortly after passing the Sainsbury's store, turn right into Flixton Road and pass Urmston station. Continue along Flixton Road then turn left at the roundabout into Chassen Road for the Abbotsfield Park; From the South: Exit the M60 at Junction 9 and turn left onto the B5158 Lostock Road. After approximately ¾ mile, turn left at the roundabout onto Crofts Bank Road (the B2514). Then as above.

VAMES MINIATURE RAILWAY

Address: Quainton Road Station,
Quainton, Aylesbury, Bucks.   HP22 4BY
Phone Nº: (01296) 655720
Year Formed: 1972
Location: Within the Buckinghamshire
Railway Centre site
Length of Line: 1,200 yards

Nº of Steam Locos: 12
Nº of Other Locos: 4
Approx Nº of Visitors P.A.: 25,000
Gauge: 3½ inches, 5 inches & 7¼ inches
Website: www.vames.co.uk
E-mail: vames.email@gmail.com

GENERAL INFORMATION

Nearest Mainline Station: Aylesbury (6 miles)
Nearest Bus Station: Aylesbury (6 miles)
Car Parking: Free parking for 500 cars available
Coach Parking: Free parking for 10 coaches
Souvenir Shop(s): Yes
Food & Drinks: Yes

SPECIAL INFORMATION

The Vames Miniature Railway is operated by
members of the Vale of Aylesbury Model
Engineering Society and is located at the
Buckinghamshire Railway Centre. Other attractions
include a 32mm and 45mm Garden Railway.

OPERATING INFORMATION

Opening Times: Sundays and Bank Holidays from
March to October inclusive. Also on Wednesdays in
the school holidays to coincide with the opening
hours of the Buckinghamshire Railway Centre.
Trains run from 10.30am to 5.30pm
Steam Working: Every operational day.
Prices: £1.50 per ride
            Under-3s travel free of charge

Detailed Directions by Car:
The Buckinghamshire Railway Centre is signposted off the A41 Aylesbury to Bicester Road at Waddesdon and off
the A413 Buckingham to Aylesbury road at Whitchurch. Junctions 7, 8 and 9 of the M40 are all close by.

VOGRIE PARK MINIATURE RAILWAY

Contact Address: Eskvalley MES,
Roslin Glen Country Park, Roslin,
Midlothian EH25 9PX
Phone N°: 07484 324614
Year Formed: 1982
Location of Line: Vogrie Country Park
Length of Line: 2,200 feet

N° of Steam Locos: 3 (Member's locos)
N° of Other Locos: 5
Approx N° of Visitors P.A.: 6,000
Gauge: 5 inches and 7¼ inches
Website: www.eskvalleymes.org.uk/vpmr
E-mail: info@eskvalleymes.org.uk

GENERAL INFORMATION

Nearest Mainline Station: Gorebridge (6.5 miles)
Nearest Bus Station: Cranston
Car Parking: Available on site
Coach Parking: Available on site
Food & Drinks: Available on site

SPECIAL INFORMATION

The Eskvalley MES operates a railway in the grounds
of the Vogrie Country Park which comprises 105
hectares of woods and Victorian parkland including
a 1876 Victorian mansion (part of which is open to
the public), a nine-hole golf course, adventure
playground and a cafeteria.

OPERATING INFORMATION

Opening Times: Sundays from Easter to September.
Trains run from 1.00pm to 5.00pm.
Steam Working: As available.
Prices: £1.00 per person per ride.
Party bookings can be arranged on other days.
Please phone Bill on 07484 324614 for further
information.

Detailed Directions by Car:
From Dalkeith: Travel South on the A68 for 2½ miles then turn right onto the B6372 signposted for Vogrie
Country Park. Continue along this road for the Park; From the A7: Travel towards Gorebridge and turn off onto
the B6372. Pass through Gorebridge staying on the B6372, continue through Newlandrig for the Park.

WELLING AND DISTRICT M.E.S.

Address: Hall Place Gardens, Bourne Road, Bexley DA5 1PQ
Year Formed: 1945
Location of Line: Eastern end of Hall Place Gardens
Length of Line: Approximately 2,000 feet

Nº of Steam Locos: Member's locos only
Nº of Other Locos: Member's locos only
Approx Nº of Visitors P.A.: Not known
Gauge: 3½ inches & 5 inches (raised track)
Website: www.wdmes.co.uk

GENERAL INFORMATION

Nearest Mainline Station: Bexley
Car Parking: Available in Hall Place car park
Food & Drinks: Hot and cold drinks plus snacks are available

SPECIAL INFORMATION

The railway operates on a site which is owned by UK Power Networks.

OPERATING INFO

Opening Times: 2024 dates: Sundays from 31st March to 2nd October. Trains run from 12.00pm to 4.00pm.
Note: Due to the National Grid building a new cable tunnel from Bexley to Woolwich, the railway was forced to relocate from Falconwood following public running days in 2019. The photo shown was taken at the previous site before the move was enforced.
Steam Working: All operating days.
Prices: £1.25 per ride.

Detailed Directions by Car:
The railway is now located in Hall Place Gardens, Bourne Road, Bexley and is right next to the A2 East Rochester Way. Approaching from the from the East, leave the A2 at the A223/A220 exit. Take the 2nd exit at the roundabout into Bourne Road, turning right after about 200 yards for Hall Place Gardens. Approaching from the West, leave the A2 at the A223/A220 exit, turn left at the roundabout and pass over the A2. Take the 3rd exit into Bourne Road at the next roundabout, turning right after about 200 yards for the Gardens.

WEST HUNTSPILL M.E.S.

Year Formed: The club was formed in the 1950s, the track was established in 1967
Length of Line: 1,062 feet (raised) and 827 feet (ground level) when complete.
Gauge: 3½ inches & 5 inches (raised track)
Location: West Huntspill Memorial Playing Fields, New Road, West Huntspill, TA9 3QE

Nº of Steam Locos: Members' locos only
Nº of Other Locos: Members' locos only
Approx Nº of Visitors P.A.: 8,000
Website: www.westhuntspillmes.co.uk
also www.facebook.com/huntspill

GENERAL INFORMATION

Nearest Mainline Station:
Highbridge (1¼ miles)
Nearest Bus Station:
Highbridge (1 mile)
Car Parking: Onsite parking available in dry weather, otherwise roadside parking only.
Souvenir Shop(s): None
Food & Drinks: Available

SPECIAL INFORMATION

Although the West Huntspill Model Engineering Society was first formed in the early 1950s, the present site was first used in 1967.

OPERATING INFO

Opening Times: 2024 dates: Every Sunday from Easter to the end of October, from 2.00pm to 4.30pm, depending on the weather.
Please check facebook for information about Special Events such as Santa Specials in December.
Steam Working: Most operating days, but dependent on which members bring in their locos.
Prices: £1.50 per ride (2 laps)
Under-5s ride free

Detailed Directions by Car:
The society's track is located on the West Huntspill Memorial Playing Field. Take the A38 and turn into New Road by West Huntspill School and the playing fields are on the left after ¼ mile.

WESTER PICKSTON RAILWAY CENTRE

Address: Wester Pickston Railway Centre, College Road, Glenalmond   PH1 3RX
Telephone Nº: (01764) 653660
Year Formed: 2002
Location: Glenalmond, near Perth
Length of Line: 2,000 metres (2,187 yards)

Nº of Steam Locos: Members' locos only
Nº of Other Locos: Members' locos only
Approx Nº of Visitors P.A.: 7,500
Gauges: 5 inches and 7¼ inches
Web site: www.smet.org.uk

GENERAL INFORMATION

Nearest Mainline Station: Perth (10 miles)
Nearest Bus Station: Perth (10 miles)
Car Parking: Free parking is available on site
Coach Parking: Available by prior arrangement
Souvenir Shop(s): None
Food & Drinks: Available

SPECIAL INFORMATION

The railway is operated by the Scottish Model Engineering Trust which was formed in 2001.

OPERATING INFORMATION

Opening Times: 2024 dates: 31st March (Easter Sunday); 26th May; 28th July and 25th August. Open from 11.30am to 4.00pm on these days. In addition, there are always members up at the track every Thursday and Sunday and visitors are welcome.
Steam Working: All open days.
Prices: £3.00 per ride or 4 rides for £10.00

Detailed Directions by Car:
From All Parts: Take the A85 from Perth to Methven and turn right onto College Road opposite the Post Office. The railway is 3 miles to the north of Methven on the right-hand side of the road.

WESTON PARK RAILWAY

Address: Weston Park, Weston-under-Lizard, Shifnal, Shropshire TF11 8LE
Telephone Nº: 07952 850336 (Railway) or (01952) 852100 (Weston Park)
Year Formed: 1980
Location of Line: Weston Park
Length of Line: Approximately 1¼ miles

Nº of Steam Locos: Variable
Nº of Other Locos: Variable
Approx Nº of Visitors P.A.: 19,500
Gauge: 7¼ inches
Website: www.weston-park.com
E-mail: info@westonrail.co.uk

GENERAL INFORMATION

Nearest Mainline Station: Shifnal (6 miles)
Nearest Bus Station: –
Car Parking: Available on site
Coach Parking: Available on site
Souvenir Shop(s): –
Food & Drinks: Available

SPECIAL INFORMATION

The railway operates in the grounds of Weston Park (www.weston-park.com), a stately home with a large park and gardens designed by 'Capability' Brown. Weston Park also has a number of other attractions for all the family.

OPERATING INFORMATION

Opening Times: 2024 dates: Most weekends in April and May and then daily from 28th May to 20th September. Trains run from 11.30am.
Steam Working: Please contact the railway for further details.
Prices: Adults £4.00
Children £4.00 (Under-2s ride for free)
Prices shown above are for train fares only. An admission charge is made for entry into the park, gardens and stately home. This admission fee is required for use of the railway. Please contact Weston Park for admission price information.
Note: The Park is closed from 15th to 18th August during the 'Camp Bestival' event.

Detailed Directions by Car:
From All Parts: Weston Park is situated by the side of the A5 in Weston-under-Lizard, Shropshire, just 3 miles from the M54 (exit at Junction 3 and take the A41 northwards) and 8 miles West of the M6 (exit at Junction 12).

WOLDIES NATURE GARDENS, TRAILS & PLAY

Address: Wintringham, Malton, North Yorkshire YO17 8HW	**Nº of Steam Locos:** None
Telephone Nº: (01944) 758641	**Nº of Other Locos:** 1
Year Formed: 2004	**Approx Nº of Visitors P.A.:** 30,000
Location of Line: Malton, N. Yorkshire	**Gauge:** 7¼ inches
Length of Line: 200 metres	**Website:** www.woldies.co.uk
	E-mail: admin@woldswaylavender.co.uk

GENERAL INFORMATION

Nearest Mainline Station: Malton (6 miles)
Nearest Bus Station: Yorkshire Coastliner Bus Service runs between Leeds, Tadcaster, Malton & Scarborough. (Tel 01653 692556). Unfortunately, there is a half a mile walk from the bus stop.
Car Parking: Free parking available on site
Coach Parking: Free parking available on site
Souvenir Shop(s): Yes
Food & Drinks: Available

SPECIAL INFORMATION

Wolds Way Lavender operates one of the few working miniature railways in the country. The train is used to bring the Lavender in from the fields to the Distillery. The train also carries the logs to fire the still in addition to the passenger carriages that are used for train rides.

OPERATING INFORMATION

Opening Times: 2024 dates: Weekends and Bank Holidays from 23rd March until Sunday 8th September and daily in July and August. Trains run from 10.00am to 4.00pm (but until 5.00pm in July and August).
Steam Working: None at present
Prices: £2.50 per ride.
Note: Admission is charged for entry to Woldies which is required to access rides but as prices vary at different times in the year, please check the website for details.

Detailed Directions by Car:
Wolds Way Lavender is half a mile off the A64 York to Scarborough road on the Scarborough side of Malton. Look out for the Brown tourist signs for Wolds Way Lavender on the main road.

WOODSEAVES MINIATURE RAILWAY

Address: Woodseaves Garden Plants, Sydnall Lane Nursery, Woodseaves, Market Drayton   TF9 2AS
Telephone Nº: (01630) 653161
Year Formed: 2004
Location of Line: Shropshire
Length of Line: Over 400 yards

Nº of Steam Locos: 2
Nº of Other Locos: 2
Approx Nº of Visitors P.A.: 1,500
Gauge: 7¼ inches
Web site: www.woodseavesminirail.co.uk
E-mail: enqs@woodseavesminirail.co.uk
Facebook: Woodseaves Miniature Railway

GENERAL INFORMATION

Nearest Mainline Station: Shrewsbury (19 miles)
Nearest Bus Station: Market Drayton (3 miles)
Car Parking: Available on site
Coach Parking: A small amount of space available
Souvenir Shop(s): None
Food & Drinks: Available in the Tea Shed

SPECIAL INFORMATION

There are two 'Woodseaves' garden centres in close proximity! Specialist Plant Nursery and Gardens Groups are welcome by prior arrangement.

OPERATING INFORMATION

Opening Times: 2024 dates: Sundays and Bank Holidays from Easter to September during afternoons from 1.30pm. Also operates on Wednesdays during school holidays.
Steam Working: Please contact the railway for further details.
Prices: £2.50
Note: Children must be accompanied by an adult and Under-2s ride for free.

Detailed Directions by Car:
From All Parts: The railway is located just off the A529 at Woodseaves, Shropshire which is situated approximately 2 miles to the south of Market Drayton.

WORTLEY TOP FORGE MINIATURE RAILWAY

Contact Address: 3 Grange Road, Royston, Barnsley   S71 4LD
Telephone Nº: (01226) 728423
Year Formed: Not known
Location of Line: Top Forge, Wortley near Thurgoland in Sheffield
Length of Line: ¼ mile

Nº of Steam Locos: Varies
Nº of Other Locos: Varies
Approx Nº of Visitors P.A.: Not known
Gauges: 7¼ inches and 5 inches
Website: www.wortleymes.com

GENERAL INFORMATION

Nearest Mainline Station: Barnsley or Sheffield
Nearest Bus Station: Barnsley
Car Parking: Available on site
Coach Parking: Available on site
Souvenir Shop(s): None
Food & Drinks: Available in the Club house

SPECIAL INFORMATION

The railway is owned by the Wortley Top Forge Model Engineers Society and runs through the grounds of the Wortley Top Forge industrial museum.

OPERATING INFORMATION

Opening Times: Sunday afternoons from Easter until November.
Steam Working: Most operating days.
Prices: Donations are welcomed.

Detailed Directions by Car:
Wortley Top Forge is situated within 10 minutes drive of the M1 motorway. From the South: Exit the M1 at Junction 35A and follow the A616 then A629 to Thurgoland; From the North: Exit the M1 at Junction 36 and follow the A61 then A616 and finally the A629 to Thurgoland. Once in Thurgoland, the forge site is ½ mile to the west of the traffic lights in the centre of the village.

WYTHALL MINIATURE STEAM RAILWAY

Address: The Transport Museum, Chapel Lane, Wythall, Birmingham, B47 6JX
Telephone Nº: (01564) 826471
Year Formed: 1980s
Location of Line: The Transport Museum, Wythall
Length of Line: 945 feet

Nº of Steam Locos: Members locos
Nº of Other Locos: Members locos
Approx Nº of Visitors P.A.: Not known
Gauge: 3½ inches, 5 inches & 7¼ inches
Website: www.wythallsteamrail.co.uk
E-mail: wythallminaturerailway@gmail.com

GENERAL INFORMATION

Nearest Mainline Station: Wythall (2 miles)
Nearest Bus Station: Birmingham (8 miles)
Car Parking: Available on site
Coach Parking: Available on site
Souvenir Shop: Yes (not specifically railway oriented)
Food & Drinks: Available on event days only

SPECIAL INFORMATION

The railway is operated by members of the Elmdon Model Engineering Society and is sited at the museum site of the Birmingham & Midland Omnibus Trust. See www.bammot.org.uk for details.

OPERATING INFORMATION

Opening Times: The Museum itself is open every weekend from Easter until the end of November. 2024 railway operating dates: 31st March; 1st April; 5th, 6th, 18th, 19th, 26th & 27th May; 15th & 16th June; 13th & 14th July; 25th & 26th August and 6th & 27th October.
Steam Working: Every operating day.
Prices: Adult Entrance Fee £8.00
            Child Entrance Fee £4.00
            Family Entrance Fee £14.00 to £20.00
Train Rides: £1.50 or £2.00
Note: The entrance fee shown for the Museum is required to access the railway.

Detailed Directions by Car:
Wythall is situated on the A435 Alcester to Birmingham road near to Junction 3 of the M42. If travelling from the South, turn left at the roundabout upon reaching Wythall and the Museum is signposted from there. Turn right at this roundabout if travelling from the North.